WHITE SILK & BLACK TAR

A Journal of the Alaska Oil Spill

Page Spencer

Forward by Margaret E. Murie

Bergamot Books
Minneapolis

Copyright © 1990 Page Spencer

All rights reserved.

First Edition
10-9-8-7-6-5-4-3-2-1

Printed in the U.S.A. on 80% recycled paper.

Cover design: Cathleen Casey
Cover photograph: McCarty Fjord, Kenai Fjords National Park
Photographer: Bud Rice
Maps and text illustrations: Elizabeth Barnard

ISBN 0-943127-04-1

Bergamot Books
PO Box 7413
Minneapolis, MN 55407
(612) 722-6058

Please write or call for a free catalog of our titles.

Appreciations

As with many things, the preparation of this book has been a process. Many people have journeyed with me during this time. I appreciate each person who touched my life as I lived with the events described here.

I appreciate the directorate of the Alaska Region of the National Park Service, especially Boyd Evison, Paul Haertel and Dave Ames, for their stand and support throughout this event, usually in the face of determined opposition. I admire Anne Castellina, Superintendent of Kenai Fjords National Park for her unswerving efforts on behalf of the park and other lands in the Seward Zone. I am indebted to Russ Kucinski who took my place in Seward and to Alex Carter for his support and understanding during my return.

I am privileged to have worked with some outstanding scientists on our voyages. I appreciate the work of each of you; may our findings survive the litigation fog so we can build a better understanding of this incredible ecosystem. I salute each person who worked on the spill with the land in their hearts. We came from many origins: government agencies, conservation groups, oil companies, the media and volunteers. We really are all in this together.

I appreciate Al Carson and Ketki for encouraging a disbelieving Page to begin writing so that I might heal, and who were only mildly smug as the journal came to be a book. I appreciate Jesse Ford who read the early pages and shared them with a friend who happens to be a publisher. I deeply appreciate Barb Wieser, Bergamot Books in its entirety, who risked her time and talent and money in the belief that this story should have a wider telling. Thank you to Linnea Carlson and Diane Solomon and all 80 llamas for the nurturing space for Barb and I to meet. I appreciate myself for the courage to tell my story in a public place.

My thanks to my parents, Dave and Eloise Spencer, who carried me into these lands before I could walk and have never left. My love and thanks to my families of birth and choice: Lynn, Bill and John Spencer, Frankie Barker, Patty Brown, Nancy Deschu and Ed Goldmann for hugs and food and encouragement and flying and expertise whenever I ask. Thanks to Paula Krebs and the *Turquoise Lady* for cruises among the icebergs.

My appreciation to my husband, Bud Rice, and to Marcia Teal, for love and logistical support throughout the evolution of this book.

This journal is an account of my personal experiences while working on the *EXXON Valdez* oil spill, and my reactions to the events as I saw them. It in no way reflects the official position of the National Park Service or any of the other agencies who were involved in the oil spill. Any factual errors are mine alone. There are many stories and truths in this event. This accounting is my story.

Page Spencer

Foreword

Page Spencer and Bud Rice were married in Anchorage in March of 1989 in a great celebration with family and friends and went off to the welcome serenity of a cabin in the Kenai mountains. It was a welcome break from their hectic work lives--Bud is the Natural Resource Specialist for Kenai Fjords National Park in Seward; Page is a scientist working for the National Park Service in their regional office in Anchorage. But when they came back, they were immediately catapulted into the news of the EXXON oil spill and the threat it posed to the land where they lived and worked and loved.

So now I ponder over this book's title, *White Silk and Black Tar*, and its deeper meaning--to Page, to Bud, to all of us.

The story begins with a survey by air with Page's brother John, when at times the fumes from the oil slick were so strong that the young scientists were nauseated, as well as horrified. Soon their lives are engulfed by 12 to 16-hour work days amidst the frightening evidence of the spreading oil spill. Page writes to me: "The magnitude of the impacts in time and space are mindboggling: contaminated waters, toxic beaches, death of birds and mammals, and the bleeding of petroleum derivatives into a pristine ecosystem far into the future."

As days pile on days and horrors upon horrors, Page begins to question her control of herself. We cannot assume that Page was the only educated and responsible person to be so affected. Hundreds of lives were affected by the seemingly insurmountable problems for people, for wildlife, for the great fisheries of Prince William Sound and for the hauntingly beautiful land and water.

We have here the true story of an earnest young scientist dealing with one of the most terrifying crises this country has ever known, a crisis which we cannot measure and which we *must not* just try to forget.

White Silk and Black Tar. There is a subtle and powerful meaning here. Will we listen? Will EXXON? Will all the agencies move strongly to prevent such an occurrence in the future? Can the people of Cordova and Seward and other towns have any hope? Can we bring back a Paradise?

What have we learned, for now and for the future?

Margaret E. Murie
January, 1990
Moose, Wyoming

Editor's Note: Margaret (Mardy) Murie, well-known conservationist and writer, grew up on the Alaska frontier at a time when travel was only possible by boat and dog sled. She spent three summers of her adolescence in Prince William Sound, exploring the bays and beaches with her stepmother in their tiny rowboat. Later she lived and traveled with her husband, the late Olaus Murie, one of America's eminent wilderness spokesmen and founder of The Wilderness Society, in the northern bush country. She chronicles her adventures in her most famous book, Two in the Far North. *Now 89 and still active in conservation causes, she lives in a log cabin on the family homestead, surrounded by the Teton wilderness.*

*To Gaia and all her otter playmates
And to Bud, who is my playmate*

KENAI FJORDS

NATIONAL PARK

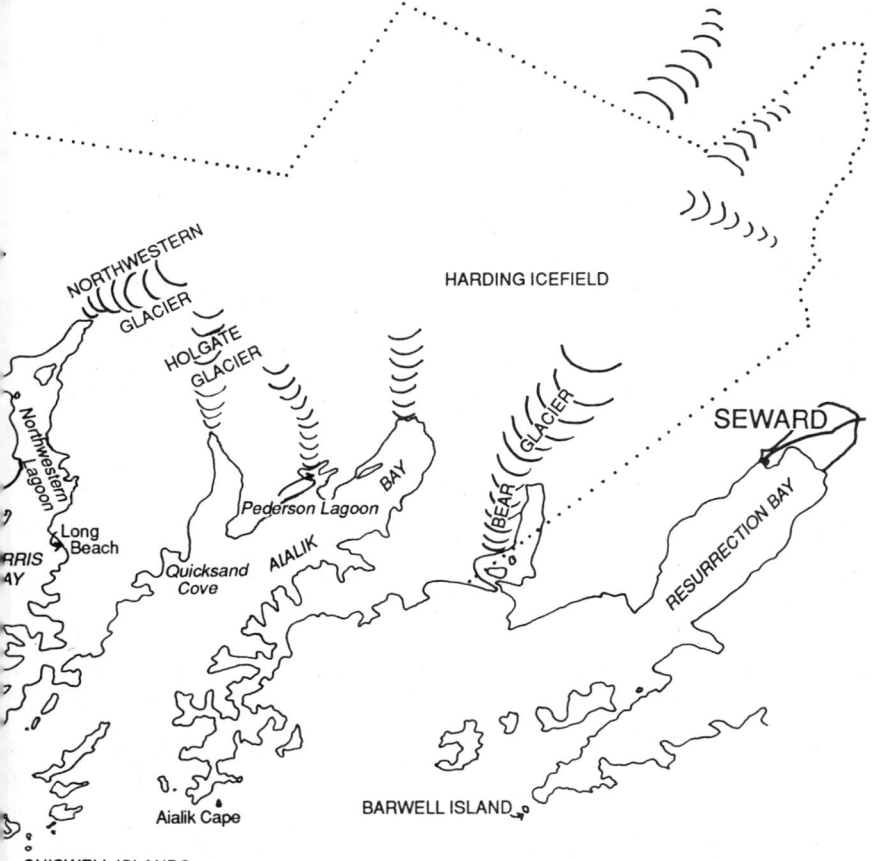

June 6, 1989
Manitoba Mountain Cabin
Kenai Mountains, Alaska

I arrived here nearly a week ago, exhausted in body, vulnerable in heart, wounded in spirit. Ravages of two months intense work in Seward on the aftermath of the oil spill. I felt disconnected from my earth source and in great pain from the destruction to the land and the energy systems that flow through her. Caught up in the insane cyclone that was created and perpetuated in Seward; crisis built on crisis until reality was gone. All of us bouncing off each other in a grey and red haze of fatigue and stress and unfelt agony. I had walked the beaches, watching the shiny black tar balls melting in the kelp and oozing toward the water like blood from wounds. Followed the bear and otter tracks along the strandline, watched the eagles feasting on oiled and rotting sea otter carcasses. Tried to count dead birds from a wing jammed in the rocks, a cleaned breastbone, a scattering of feathers stuck to boulders and logs by oil and blood. Tried to play God beach by beach, naming coves for cleaning, leaving others in silence because cleaning is too damaging or simply not possible. Tears mingled with sunset waves at the end of each day as I attempted to reconcile the stunning sunlight mountains and sparkling icebergs with the invasion of humans and tar.

Back in town, I tried to design and implement and integrate a program to track oiling and monitor impacts for the entire ecosystem. But I had no place to work. Phones came and went and changed numbers hourly, furniture moved daily, computers were fought over, and work was lost when they were unplugged. Dozens of noisy people swirled about in chaos; energy and egos ricochetting off each other. Everyone swept along on an adrenaline rush. The entire system was out of control, a reflection of the death throes in the Sound, in the fjords, in the Straits, on down the coast as far as the currents and wind will reach.

Bud and I began our marriage in this maelstrom. We bought a house and tried to move in. Attempted to make a home, to live together in a setting neither of us had ever envisioned. But I felt homeless, living out of a duffel bag and car, my possessions spread between three residences. I try to remember our wedding, our vows to each other. "Remember this day in hard times. . . ." I look at pictures over and over again, trying to find myself in them. I can't relate to the joyous woman in sparkling white silk. Try to find my serene companion in the frazzled man who is being pulled in a hundred different directions. I hold the jewels that adorned my hair, and cannot recapture the hope of that day.

Somehow it felt like sooner or later the focus of many of the crises came down to Bud or I or both of us. No other park people know the land like Bud does, no one else has walked the beaches as I have. Work and demands piled higher and higher. Ten hours, twelve, fifteen, sometimes eighteen hours a day. I tried to find or make pockets of sanity or serenity in this swirling madness. I felt like a fireweed seed in a firestorm. I watched myself being swept downstream, whirling, ineffective, without center, without stability. Pushed into rocks, over falls, twirled in whirlpools and ejected again. Frantically reaching for eddies, each one snatched away as I came alongside. Until finally one night I heard someone say very gently: "Page, someone else can do it for awhile."

And so I came to this cabin for a time of rest and quiet. I have been here a week now and have to go to town to make a phone call. I've slept a lot, ten to twelve hours each night. Still plagued by nightmares of the oil spill. Read a lot, mostly to escape. Hiked some. Bud came for a couple nights and a day, and we enjoyed a run on a new trail together. Found a large garden of forget-me-nots on the Devil's Pass trail. Split some wood. Yesterday I went to Skilak Lake and followed the shore to a sheltered cove where I built a fire and sat a long time. Inland sea--waves and gulls, but no tide or salt or oil. I feel a very fragile reconnection to my land again. Born of wind and firesmoke and spring flowers and sifting rain.

*March 30, 1989
Anchorage, Alaska*

A phone call from my brother John starts it: "would I like to take a flight over Prince William Sound and the *EXXON Valdez* this afternoon?" I am recently back at work, just beginning to become deeply involved in my new job as reclamation specialist for the National Park Service in Alaska. Field work schedules for visiting placer mines next summer are put on hold as I arrange for the afternoon off, grab charts and camera, and call the FAA for a weather briefing. Anchorage Flight Service advises high overcast and calm winds, with a restricted zone 3000-feet high and one mile in radius around the grounded tanker, *EXXON Valdez*.

This is my third day back in the office after my honeymoon. Bud Rice and I were married on March 18 and joined friends and family for a joyous reception at my brother's hangar the next day. Five days later on March 24th, while we were on our honeymoon ski trip in the Kenai Mountains, the super tanker *EXXON Valdez* strayed out of the shipping lane in Prince William Sound and fetched up hard aground on Bligh Reef. Eight of her eleven fully loaded cargo tanks were ripped open, and over 11 million gallons of unrefined crude oil gushed into the pristine waters of Prince William Sound like a fountain. Pushed by winds and pulled by currents, the dark poison tendrils spread through the straits and passages and reached for the shores of this magnificent glacier-carved land.

John keeps his plane on the airstrip near the small resort town of Girdwood, at the head of Turnagain Arm. After grabbing lunch, survival gear and cameras, I drive out the arm to meet him and friends John Grimmett and Cathy Frost. We preflight the plane and lift off. Our first destination is to pick up Bud at Seward, another small town at the northern end of Resurrection Bay and the southern terminus of the

Alaska Railroad. Bud lives in Seward, where he works for the Kenai Fjords National Park as the Natural Resource Specialist.

I take the wheel from the right seat, flying east up the arm. Skimming the shoulders of the mountains in the sun, watching early signs of breakup below us. We go along the railroad track up the Placer River and through the pass to Trail Lake. I get some photos of the country; Bud and I had talked of a ski trip from Moose Pass to Portage, but he hasn't seen the land yet. At Cooper Landing we swing over Grant Lake so Cathy can get a view. Usually I fly the family's Piper Supercruiser, a sort of overgrown supercub. It is a fabric and frame butterfly--small, light and responsive. The four-place Cessna 180 seems heavy and sluggish in my hands as we bank around the end of the lake next to the mountains. I'll have to get used to flying with two hands if I fly her often. As we descend to Bear Lake at Seward, John takes over. The snow on the lake surface is wind blown, very hard and rough, and the 180 bounces and clatters over the drifts to a stop.

Bud is waiting for us at the south end of the lake, festooned with cameras and a handful of maps. He throws his pack in the cargo compartment and climbs into a back seat. As John taxis the plane out for take off, Bud and I clasp hands, smoothing the new rings on each other's fingers. This is the first time we have seen each other since we came out of Upper Russian Lake from our honeymoon. We fly south down Resurrection Bay, meeting a C-130 nearly nose to nose by Fox Island. Crossing through a low pass, we continue east across Day Harbor. The day is bright with the high overcast moving in from the south. To the north the sky is clear, and the mountains stand shining against the sky. We make a couple passes over my brother Bill's cabin at Horsehead Lake. All seems intact. This is the first time any of us have been here since it was built last fall. The cabin is snuggled up to the cliff at the storm tide line, and we wondered how well it would survive the winter storms. We follow the coast east along the cliffs and bays to Point Puget. Here we see a pod of sea lions just offshore. They are crowded together in the water and appear to be a whorl of drift logs. As we pass over, one or two lift their heads, but mostly we are ignored.

Oil has been reported in Prince William Sound as far south as Knight Island and moving into Montague Passage. This is day six of the spill, and as yet there is very little being done to collect the oil or stop its spread through Prince William Sound. The news is sporadic and low key. Attitudes seem to vary between "it's no big deal" to "it's too big to handle." In any event, there is little equipment or action forthcoming. As we fly along, we watch for possible signs of oil, but we're not sure what it will look like. Brown scum is washing against the cliffs, but we finally decide it's tidal detritus.

The lower coast of the Kenai Peninsula west of Prince William Sound seems pristine as ever. We see no boat or plane traffic as we fly along Johnstone Bay, Point Puget and across lower Port Bainbridge. Several icebergs are floating offshore as we swing up Port Bainbridge and across the island to Port Ashton. The visual quiet of the coast is jarred by the activity at the hatchery in Sawmill Bay. The buildings are tucked into the back side of the bay, while the water in front of the hatchery is a beehive of activity. Three lines of bright yellow boom are stretched across the entrance, like garlands between rocks and islands. Boats zip back and forth, drawing frothy wakes parallel with the booms. We dodge a helicopter, watch for aircraft. Float planes nose up to the boom and dock like nursing puppies. The oil line is not here yet, but frantic preparations are underway. We circle once, then move northeast. As we approach the southern end of Knight Island, we see a dark line stretching from Knight Island toward Montague Island. Behind it the sea lies calm; before it breezes ruffle the surface. John circles, descending until we're less than 50 feet above the shore and flies north along Knight Island.

This is our first close exposure to the crude oil from the *EXXON Valdez*. The tide is about midway out and there is a thick line of oil along the high tide mark. The stench of petroleum fills the plane, making us nauseous. The oil lies thick on the water right up to the shoreline. On the windward shore here, it appears to be several inches thick and has a polygonal cracking pattern over the surface. It is pitch black, with a dull sheen. The normal surf action is subdued, almost gentle. Mariners have long known that oil will calm the surface of stormy waters. Now the beaching surf is damped down and barely ripples at the shore. Off to the east and northeast across the water, the oil extends as far as we can see, at least to Montague Island. We fly up the beach of Knight Island. In some places the water currents have formed swirls in the oil cover, a paisley of thick black along the shore. Boulders and steep cliffs have a ring on the rocks. In small coves the oil is pushed up into the corners, around every rocky islet, brushing every little beach. The darkened current has spread into the Bay of Isles; white snow, dark green hemlocks, black tide line. Off to the east we can see fishing boats headed south. Instead of the usual white wake, their passing is marked by a dissipating wedge where water shows through the oil cover. As we proceed north along Knight Island, we spot two cleanup crews in coves. Eight or ten people in orange suits huddle together above the high tide line; no one appears to be doing anything on the oiled beach.

Between Eleanor and Naked Islands we see two skimmers working in the vastness of the oil. Hundreds of square miles of oil and these tiny triangles of boats and boom attempting to collect some of the millions of gallons of crude oil. The crippled tanker takes shape to the northeast. A second tanker is rafted on its south side. The remaining 40 million gallons on the *EXXON Valdez* are being offloaded before it can be moved off the reef. Leaking booms surround both vessels. We make a couple passes over the tankers, clearly reading the name of the *EXXON Valdez* on the bow. Helicopters whirl by, a Lear jet whips south. A flock of Columbia Glacier icebergs floats loose to the northwest. Turning 180 degrees to the southeast, I see 14 additional tankers waiting offshore for their turn up Valdez Arm. They look like vultures crouched on the horizon.

We fly up over Heather Island and the face of the Columbia Glacier. The dazzling pure white of the snow and blue and white of the ice are a stunning contrast to the spreading blackness we just left. Swinging through a small pass, we land on Miners Lake in Unakwik Inlet. The sky is clear here and the sun blinding bright off the surrounding snow. All five of us punchhole down to the inlet shore through a small draw. Tide still low. Fragments of ice are herded up near the rocky beach, sounding like delicate swishing silk and tinkling crystal as the berglets brush against each other. A pair of ducks dive and play across the cove. The sun is hot as we walk along the water's edge. I carefully examine the shoreline, noting the usual winter scarcity of kelps and mollusks in the intertidal zone. Already my mind is wrestling with the job of analyzing the impacts from the oil spill. I realize we know very little about the rhythms of these lands at this time of year. Later we all sprawl in the warm dry beach ryegrass and fall asleep in the sun. I am still nauseous from the petroleum fumes and am beginning to feel the first effects of the overwhelming disaster which is underway out in the Sound.

The sun is warm on my face as I lay cushioned with the husks of last summer's grasses. I feel shocked and numbed by what I have just seen. This is land I have climbed in the sunshine, a thousand bonsai gardens laid out by the glaciers. Like most people, I felt only mild alarm when I first heard about the oil spill on the radio news while driving back to Anchorage three days ago. The oil industry in Alaska had made prolonged and repeated assurances that they could handle any spill which might occur. They even had conducted practice oil spills in Valdez Arm, using thousands of oranges to simulate crude oil. I had chuckled to think of the sea otters playing with the oranges, rolling them in their paws, pouncing on the bright orbs as they tossed in the waves, trying to break the fruits open by pounding the oranges on rocks held on their chests. So I had thought that the full might of worldwide cleanup operations would immediately be brought to bear if all precautions failed, and somehow, oil was released into the environment. But the last hour's flight has shattered that illusion. The tiny skimmers stretched out in the slick, the idle crews on the rocks, the leaking boom surrounding the *EXXON Valdez* are only futile gestures in the face of the suffocating blanket of death spread out in the sea.

I have spent most of my life in this land. My parents homesteaded on Beaver Creek, near the fishing village of Kenai, and raised four lively children there. Dad worked for the Fish and Wildlife Service, first with the Kenai National Moose Range, and later with all the wildlife refuges in Alaska. Although we built our home and lived a semi-subsistence lifestyle, there was lots of time for exploring the mountains, lakes, rivers and coasts of southcentral Alaska. Many Friday nights, the weekend project would be put on hold, and we would scurry to pack for an adventure, on skis or by foot, in canoes or in the small sailboat Dad had built. I grew up with a backyard of millions of acres, moving freely and confidently in the wilderness. Later I had gone Outside to school in Colorado, to earn the academic pedigree that would allow me to make a profession of learning about the land and helping to manage human activities on it. Now I bring together the richness of both sides--the professional ecologist and my long history here--and try to meld these parts into a whole that can understand the patterns and processes of this land I call home.

John stirs first, waking us back to the reality of passing time and miles to go. Slowly, still dazed by the sun, we make our way back to the plane and take off. A detour brings us along the face of Unakwik Glacier. Ice columns tower over us as John flies below the ice level. Further out we see seals basking in the sun on icebergs. We fly down the inlet and over to Perry Island. Oil has hit the east and south sides of the island. We are all quiet as I take the wheel to fly back to Girdwood through Portage Pass. I need something else to occupy my mind and flying a new plane takes my concentration. We land at Girdwood about 6:00 P.M. Bud and I leave immediately to drive to Seward.

I find it difficult to collect and express my feelings. A light veil of grief and pain drifts over me. Bud is in shock and has the first stirrings of anger. These are the harbingers of emotions which will later overwhelm and drive us. But for now, we turn to science. It is obvious to both of us that the oil will come to Kenai Fjords National Park. The oil slick is moving rapidly south to Montague Straits, where it will be loosed in the Gulf of Alaska. The Alaska Coastal Current flows east to west along the northern curve of the Gulf, and the flow will carry the oil to the lower coast of the Kenai Peninsula. Four hundred miles of this intricate coastline are in Kenai Fjords National Park. The Alaska Maritime National Wildlife Refuge is a scattering of offshore islands. West of the National Park is the outer coast of Kachemak Bay State Wilderness Park.

We discuss and design the work that would need to be done to assess the impacts which may accrue to the fjord ecosystem from oil. We list known sources of data, previous research. Identify what needs to be done quickly to provide data from the pre-oiled environment for comparison. Sort out what may be feasible in the short time available to us.

The magnitude of the impacts of the oil spill over time and across space are mindboggling. Bud and I review the obvious effects first: contaminated water, toxic beaches, death of individual birds and animals. Then like links in a horrible chain, we go on to longer and longer term effects: bleeding of petroleum derivatives into the ecosystem for years from oil deposits in gravel and sands; impenetrable pavement-like surface on flow-through beaches; the changes in the intertidal and near-tidal vegetation communities; impacts to populations of plankton, small fish, big fish, bottom fish; concentration of toxins in the flesh of mussels and accumulation of hunger and toxic materials on up through the food chain--whales, sea lions, sea otters, land otters, sea birds, eagles, wolverines, bears.

The impacts of the oil will flow through the entire ecosystem, following the transformation of energy and nutrients. The crude oil will change shape and composition, but will remain for a very long time. After the illness and death of individuals, there will be long term effects on populations and community composition. Reproductive and survival success will change, food supplies will be altered. The energy balance of the entire system has been drastically altered. Although an equilibrium will eventually be established, it will be different than before. We do not even begin to discuss the significance of the loss of a pristine wilderness system, the impacts which will accrue to humans in economic, emotional and spiritual terms.

It is late when we reach Seward. As we enter a local restaurant for a quick supper, it is crowded with the first wave of people coming to work on the oil spill. Many are local people, already mobilizing against the threat of oil off the Seward shores. I see people I have known from the Alaska Fire Service when I worked for the Bureau of Land Management. Dave Liebersbach tells us that he is heading up an Incident Command Team (ICT) which the National Park Service has called into Seward to help handle the operation of responding to the oil spill. I am so tired and overwhelmed that I still cannot truly grasp the enormity of the situation. Bud and I get to his home late and tumble into bed. I am up very early the next morning to drive back to my office in Anchorage for work.

March 31

I move through the day in a haze. Meetings are held to update us on the status of the oil spill and the Park Service's intended course of action. The experience from the flight and the research outline Bud and I developed on our drive to Seward are already being put to use. When they ask for volunteers to assist with the work, I offer to go and late in the afternoon I am told to report to Seward the next day.

Normally, the 125-mile drive from Anchorage to Seward takes about two and a half hours. The highway skirts Turnagain Arm, then climbs into the mountains over two passes before descending through a canyon to Seward. During daylight with good weather, it is one of the most spectacular routes in Alaska. But in the dark or bad weather, it is a twisting treacherous road. I drive down late that night, dead tired. It is the most difficult trip I've ever had to Seward and I nearly fall asleep. With the window down and the radio on full blast, I finally make the last 30 miles sometime after midnight.

April 1

Up early this morning. The ICT has set up headquarters in a U.S. Forest Service house in Seward. They are specifically trained to bring order and get things accomplished in crisis situations where the usual government procedures would become hopelessly bogged down. Usually they are on wild fires, but they begin to adapt to deal with the unusual situation here.

We only have a few days before the leading edge of the oil slick will sweep along the outer coast of the park. In these precious days, we need to make collections and observations of conditions before the oil arrives. Bud takes responsibility for identifying and coordinating these pre-oiling assessment voyages, beginning to implement the design we developed two days ago. Logistics are arranged, equipment and people located, and the whole operation swings into action. I know Bud wants to go with one of the trips but his knowledge of park lands and resources is unique and invaluable. He has spent seven years in the park, four of the summers as a backcountry ranger on the outer coast, and mapped the glacial changes for his Master's thesis work. A week before our wedding, he finished writing the oil spill contingency plan for the park. As part of the plan, he also developed a map of the park which shows the areas of major resource concentration and use. Hundreds of questions and requests come at him: what should we do, where should we do it, how? Even non-park people find him: locations of salmon spawning streams, where to boom, how much boom will it take, strength of currents, place for boom tie-downs? Thousands of big and small details.

The previous day, there was a short trip in Resurrection Bay south of Seward to inventory sea birds and mammals. A longer trip is planned for sea birds and mammals along the entire coast of the park and the islands of the Alaska Maritime National Wildlife Refuge. Another trip will be responsible for describing and sampling terrestrial vegetation, soils, water quality, plankton and fisheries along the coasts of the park. I am appointed to lead this trip. Other voyages will inventory beaches, remove winterkill carcasses and assess recreation use; collect data in the intertidal zone for vegetation, animals, and sediments; and conduct aerial surveys for birds and marine mammals. Energy is high, but focused on specific goals, and the operation runs much more smoothly than I would expect given the circumstances.

The boat trip I lead is scheduled to leave for four days that afternoon. The *Shaman* has been leased for the trip from Kenai Fjords Tours. We hurriedly put together a crew of scientists: myself and Mike Tetreau for the vegetation and soils; Sandy Milner and Shelly Williams for the water, plankton, and fisheries. I rapidly put together a design for the vegetation work and equipment. There is still snow cover above the high tide line, so we'll come back later to collect data. At this point I just need to establish some representative plots and develop general descriptions of the near-tidal vegetation communities. Bud lists areas of prime concern for wildlife habitat and fisheries.

We scatter in all directions to locate equipment and gear. Iron ribar rods, measure tapes, paint and tags to mark plots, my plant identification book, notebooks, cameras, film, binoculars . . . I scurry to Bud's apartment to ransack my duffel bags, pulling out field clothes and a good book. In the midst of all this I squeeze in a couple hours to do my income tax return and mail it off. I head back into town to make a grub list and buy the food. I wheel up and down the grocery aisles, grabbing stuff and hoping there are no finicky eaters in the crew. Then I realize I don't have enough of my thyroid medication to last the trip, run down a doctor and get a prescription filled. The matter of dinghies takes much time and discussion. We finally locate a nine-foot aluminum skiff much the worse for wear and take Shelly's small inflatable Avon. Neither is very satisfactory, but they are all we can find on short notice. The park doesn't have enough survival suits for all of us, and again we raid Shelly's personal warehouse. Survival suits are designed to keep us alive and afloat if we have to abandon ship in the frigid waters of the Gulf. Without them the prognosis for surviving is about 15 minutes. In the meantime, Eric, the captain of the *Shaman*, is dewinterizing the vessel and trying to locate a crewmember. By late afternoon we have assembled most of the gear, but a glitch in the water pump on the *Shaman* delays departure. By the time the pump is fixed, there is insufficient daylight to make the run to Aialik Bay, so I postpone leaving until early next morning. The ICT wanted the record to show that this voyage left on April 1st, even if we only went five miles down the bay and anchored for the night. I promise to be gone before sunrise. The political pressures have already begun to clash with practical considerations. It is again very late when Bud and I finally get home, and we crawl into bed with little to say.

April 2

We're assembled by 5:30 A.M., but the sky is pitch black and full of stars. We all forgot that the switch to Daylight Savings time occurred that night, thus delaying sunrise by an hour. By 7:00 A.M. we have cast off and headed out. Very faint light over the eastern mountains and calm seas as we motor out into Resurrection Bay. Resurrection Bay is one of the large fjords which indent the southern coast of the Kenai Peninsula. The main bay is mitten-shaped; Seward is located at the finger tips, and Bear Glacier butts the shore where the thumb would stick north. Numerous coves are stuck into the sides of the bay, some with small beaches and short valleys behind them. Mountains rise up from the water surface and extend deep below the fjords to the ocean floor. The waterline of the ocean is arbitrary here, located by sea level and not any feature of the land. The lower mountain slopes are wrapped in thick spruce and hemlock forest, thinning out to dense alder thickets at about 2000 feet, and rising to alpine tundra, rocks and glaciers. This early in the year snow still covers most of the slopes, although early waterfalls are tumbling down the draws. Avalanches frequently run to the ocean, leaving thick snowbanks at the water's edge. Looking south, a flotilla of islands protrude near the eastern side of the bay. Beyond the headlands of Capes Resurrection and Aialik, the Gulf of Alaska stretches into the Pacific Ocean.

The *Shaman* is the boat used for the Resurrection Bay tours in the summer. She is 53-feet long and seems luxurious for our crew of six. Randy Upton is the crewman; Eric Olson the captain. The sun rises as we motor south, golden rosy light on the western peaks, then first sun as we round the point to Bear Glacier. There are Dall porpoises for a few minutes in the bow wake and bald eagles in trees along the shore. We see a pair of whales; Minke or possibly grey whales in migration. After the frantic activity of the previous three days, it is a real relief to be out on the water. It is cold, but I sit on the bow trying to calm down and focus on the land and the task ahead of me.

My plan is to make a rapid reconnaissance around the coast of the park, emphasizing the important habitat areas Bud identified. We will move east to west, checking the major fjords which reach into the mountains. The first one is Aialik Bay with several tidewater glaciers, Pederson Lagoon and important rookery islands for seabirds and sea lions. We'll bypass Harris Bay and Northwestern Lagoon on the way out, heading west for Nuka Bay, composed of McCarty Fjord, Beauty Bay, Surprise Bay and North Arm. These deep bays have critical habitat areas and streams, as well as spectacular scenery, protected waters for kayaks and small boats, and unique geologic features. The whole region is capped by the Harding Icefield. Over 30 glaciers drip off the icefield and into the fjords like soft frosting off warm cinnamon buns. Time and weather permitting on the return trip, we will poke into other bays--Taroka, Paguna, Thunder and Black--and swing by some of the offshore islands. We cannot even hope to make a thorough examination of the country for vegetation, soil, water, fisheries and plankton. But the spot checking we do will be the first in this land for this season, and we can integrate it with other work to follow.

As we proceed up Aialik Bay toward Pederson Lagoon, we encounter thick brash ice from the glaciers at the head of the bay. Eric maneuvers carefully for awhile, but the ice becomes too thick and we anchor up about a mile from the lagoon entrance. We launch the aluminum skiff, dubbed the *Tin Lizzy*, and put the three-horse outboard engine on her. All four of us pile in, then hand down equipment. Fortunately it's pretty stable, because there is very little freeboard. We weave through the ice to the long beach south of the lagoon, where Sandy and Shelley get out to walk. Mike and I continue to the entrance of the lagoon, where the tide is flowing out fairly strongly and a couple of sea lions are fishing in the standing waves. As we approach the outlet, the large bull eyes us curiously, then swims closer. Shouts and waving arms do not deter him; with each surfacing he is closer yet. I consider grabbing the aerosol can of cayenne "hot sauce" we carry for bears, but Mike finally gets the skiff turned around. The sea lion is much larger than the skiff and certainly heavier. Neither Mike nor I relish the idea of swimming with the icebergs and sea lions that day.

Mike leaves me on the outside beach of the lagoon and goes back to pick up Sandy and Shelley. I walk around the inside shore of the lagoon. The snow is still deep above the high tide line, with litter of beach ryegrass and sedges on the fringes. Otter tracks thread between the water and snow. It is very quiet, only a few birds, and no wind. The sun is bright, but not warm. I am dressed in multiple layers of polypropylene, bunting and wind proofing. I come to an area that is flooded by high tides. Scrapes in the mud show where icebergs drag along with the tide. The vegetation types grow in definite lines with respect to tidal flooding. I lay out two vegetation plots and collect soil samples. These are to verify that there is no oil in the soil prior to arrival of the oil from the *EXXON Valdez*. The tide is flowing in after Mike joins me. Our radios aren't working, but we finally get the attention of the water crew who are collecting samples in the lagoon. They come to pick us up, and we all move to the stream at the north end of the lagoon. Sandy and Shelley go upstream looking for evidence of salmon fry. Still too early in the season; the creek is dry just a short distance upstream.

We all re-embark in *Tin Lizzy* for the trip across the lagoon and out to the *Shaman*. We make it over the shallow bar at the outlet, then are caught in the tidal outpouring from the lagoon. We whirl around the corner and buck the standing waves, noting with relief that the sea lions have moved on. The brash ice is even thicker now, and the current shoves *Tin Lizzy* forcefully into the slush and bergs. As ice closes around us, at least we are upright and slowed down. Shelley and Sandy each take an oar and lie on the bow, and Mike is the tiller man. I lay low to keep the center of gravity down. We slowly start working our way back to the *Shaman*, following narrow leads in the ice, using the oars to push bergs out of the way. Back and forth we maneuver, trying to find clear channels, only to have the ice push across and close us off. The ice also moved in around the *Shaman*, so Eric has had to move downbay another mile while we were in the lagoon. By radio he tries to direct us to clearer paths, but neither of us is high enough to see very well. The tidal current is carrying us further out into the middle of the bay, along with our ice walls. It is a beautiful sunny afternoon, but we don't properly appreciate the sparkling ice. After a tense hour and a half, we finally approach the *Shaman* and gladly climb up onto the spacious decks. Then Eric has another half hour of careful maneuvering as he moves the *Shaman* out of the ice surrounding her. Finally we are in clear water again and motor down to Quicksand Cove.

Quicksand Cove has a long sand beach at its head with a summer lagoon behind the beach. The stream is not open to the ocean now but probably flows out during summer. No sign of dead winterkill on the beach. The south end has a stand of spruce and hemlock which is occasionally inundated by storm tides. Lots of land otter tracks; evidence of at least two romping and rolling in the sand. The otter and raven tracks are woven in an intricate pattern between snow line and water. I establish a plot in the beach ryegrass at the edge of the snow and Sandy checks the drainage for salmon fry. The sun slips down behind the rim of mountains as we finish our reconnaissance.

We take a quick run out to the Chiswell Islands to check reports of oil. No visible sign of oil there, but the smell of petroleum is strong. There are about 200 sea lions hauled out on the rookery, seven or eight immature bald eagles, and we sight spouts of seven whales. We run back to Verdant Cove in the last light and anchor for the night. Randy cooks steak dinner for us in the tiny galley. We all sack out shortly after cleaning up.

I have made my way through this long day by focusing on immediate and ordinary tasks. The odyssey in the brash ice seems more real than the mirage of disaster in the gasoline fumes at the Chiswell Islands. It is too overwhelming to allow my mind to absorb the significance of the fumes and the horrifying specter of death borne along the coast by the current.

April 3

I am awakened abruptly at 6:30 A.M. by the alarm of the diesel engines starting near my head. Soon there is the whine of the winch, the rattle of the anchor chain, and then the soothing throb of engines and the gentle rise and fall of the hull on swells. There is something very nurturing about the rhythm of the engine and swells, and I rest half asleep/half awake for awhile. Soon though, I am up and take hot chocolate to the pilot house as we go through Granite Passage, the narrow waterway between Granite Island and Harris Peninsula. The shores of Granite Island rise steep and smooth and black in the grey morning light. Several sharp coves indent the shore of Harris Peninsula off the starboard side.

It is another bright cold day with high overcast and a gentle swell from the south. We cruise close to the shore along the outer coast, watching for wildlife and birds in the area. Wildlife is pretty sparse except for whales; we see spouts of at least seven. Steam bursts white above the grey rolling swells, fading away downwind, then rising again with another surfaced breath. Although we watch closely, we see no recognizable signs of oil along the shores. This stretch of the outer coast is spectacular. Sheer bedrock cliffs plunge over 2000 feet into the ocean. Convoluted patterns in the rock show early pressures and distant origins. Slanting ledges are mountain goat trails, and vegetation is sparse patches of battered spruce and alder along avalanche tracks. Surf pounds on the narrow gravel beaches, hanging onto the edge of the cliffs by their toenails. Nothing breaks the ocean until Hawaii and then Antarctica. At several points the cliffs are fractured by deep indented bays, reaching back into the mountains. These offer the only shelter along here, places where the glaciers carved through the bedrock weakness. We make the quick run through McArthur Pass, watching for drift logs which accumulate at the east end, and then into the calm waters of lower McCarty Fjord.

Our objectives for the day are the rich lagoons on either side of the fjord, just outside the shallow moraine, a ridge of till left by the glacier. We anchor outside James Lagoon first. There is less snow in McCarty Fjord than we saw yesterday in Aialik Bay. Today we wise up and take both skiffs for the run into James Lagoon. Sandy and Shelley take the inflatable Avon with oars, and we tow them into the lagoon with *Tin Lizzy*. Fortunately, the tide is at slack high, so we have no trouble getting in. James Lagoon is a peaceful sea lake, closed off from the fjord by a large morainal beach and surrounded by mountains. An immature bald eagle flaps slowly by, coming to rest in one of the spruce above the rocky shore. We count at least 25 sea otters inside, some feeding in the tidal inflow at the entrance, and others on their backs in various stages of repose. At the head of the bay we startle a river otter near the shore.

The head of this lagoon sank during the big earthquake in 1964, leaving a large stand of dead cottonwood and spruce snags above a salt marsh cut by several tidal channels. This area is good habitat for black bear and river otter and supports runs of pink and chum salmon. Mike and I pull *Tin Lizzy* into one of the channels and tie off to a snag. We establish three plots to represent the main near-tidal vegetation types in the area. They range from a dense grass, sedge and beach ryegrass stand to an area of very sparse goose greens which is good feeding ground for bears and geese. We collect a soil sample and document all with photos and sketches. Some of these plots will be tricky to relocate in summer after the vegetation grows high. The tide has turned while we are doing our exploring. We motor towards the water crew to check in, but Sandy is rowing strongly to a new sample site, and we barely catch up at the far end of the lagoon. Wind and tide are in his favor, but he moves at an impressive speed, and we resolve to not let him have the engine-equipped skiff anymore. As Mike and I head back out toward the *Shaman* the tide is flowing out of the lagoon at a brisk pace. We are pulled into the current, and whirlpools reach for the edge of *Tin Lizzy* as we are slammed out into the fjord. For a heart-stopping instant, we tilt and start to revolve into a whirlpool, but Mike gets her straightened, and we overshoot the *Shaman* on our way out. At least this time, I would only be swimming with sea otters if we go over. We warn the water people about the perils of the exit, but they do fine in the inflatable. *Tin Lizzy* is starting to get a bad name for herself.

We get people and skiffs back on board the *Shaman*, and Eric follows the outer curve of the submerged moraine across the fjord to McCarty Lagoon and Delight Spit. Delight Creek and Lake support a red salmon run, providing good habitat for bears and kayakers during salmon season. Delight Spit is a popular camping location, two miles of beautiful sand beach surrounded by spectacular mountains. Last summer Bud and I watched three humpback whales feeding up and down in front of the moraine, which is just off the Delight beach. The moraine nearly reaches the sea surface 700 feet off the fjord floor and was built by McCarty Glacier over thousands of years.

We put the water people ashore and send them up the creek to look for salmon fry. Mike and I explore the snag forest for good plot locations. The area floods during higher tides, and little grows there except goose greens, some sparse grass and a strange lichen-like green algae. Doesn't look like much to me, but Bud has reported heavy bear use in the area.

While working on this plot a Beaver circles overhead several times, and Mike comes running to me for a radio relay from the *Shaman*. Literally out of the blue, I get an order to be picked up so I can go to Valdez and relieve the Department of Interior representative for the oil spill to set up centers for coordination and bird rehabilitation. But I am dismayed at the thought of going to manage birds and politics in the same breath. "I don't do ducks!" I blurt to a puzzled Eric, who attempts to relay the message to Bud in the Beaver. Agitated, I pace the beach waiting for the radio relay. Apparently a light goes on in the plane overhead, and I finally get a message back that they will find someone else. Good--right now I want to be an ecologist on the land, not a bureaucrat in chaos. Normally I would accept such a task, but for now I want a calmer job. The Beaver climbs over the mountains to the east, and quiet settles on the fjord again. Shaken, I locate another plot in the beach ryegrass, and Mike and I note evidence of campers on the spit.

Mike and I walk the Delight beach to check other camp spots and winterkill. We make rattles from the dried bulbs of bull kelp and pebbles and play jazz rhythms as we walk along. The beach is long and clean, and the winter storms have swept over the beach ridge and cleaned the sloping dunes behind. The sky has cleared up and I can almost imagine the sun is warm. A seal follows along with us offshore, and we see a lot of land otter tracks. They seem to have so much fun, running and whirling in the loose sand with each other. There are two kinds of otters on the coast: sea otter and land or river otter. Sea otter are mainly marine animals, living most of their lives in the sea, eating prodigious quantities of fish and shellfish. Land otters are versatile, living in inland lakes or rivers and equally at home along the coast. They move easily between land and water, feeding mainly on fish and carrion. And to human perceptions, land otters play. They build mud slides down stream banks into deep pools, whirl and sprint and tumble in the sand, curiously inspecting toys of shells and pebbles. These otter tracks scamper along the beach as if in celebration of the advent of spring and the return of flowing water.

In some ways, this work feels very ordinary. I'm in familiar lands, though at an unusual season. The work is similar to what I've done before, trying to figure out the components of an ecosystem and their interactions. But overshadowing the ordinariness is an impending sense of massive and erratic change. As I look out into the Gulf of Alaska I feel like there is a dark cloud on the horizon. Winterclean beaches, spring sunlight, and the knowledge that the oil is headed this way. All the natural changes and human pressures rolled into one event, about to arrive on the night tide.

The sun goes down before the *Shaman* returns for us, and we decide to row out to keep warm. We're well offshore when the *Shaman* finally comes alongside to pick us up, but I see the tops of kelp just below the hull. When I step into the pilot house the fathometer reads eight feet--and the *Shaman* draws six. We move down to Midnight Cove for the night. A quiet evening in the deep and protected anchorage.

April 4

Again this morning we're underway before sun and scientists are up, and I snuggle into my sleeping bag for a few extra cradle-like minutes. But this is short lived; Beauty Bay is just a quick run away and we have good weather again. In Beauty Bay Mike and I choose to be dropped off and picked up rather than walk the beach both ways. Randy shuttles us ashore, and we slog across the extensive mud flats to the beach.

There is a large stand of snags here too, more remnants from the 1964 earthquake, and deep snow above the high tide line. We set out a plot in the sparse sedges at the top of the tidal zone, then explore the rest of the beach. I wander back into the mature spruce forest, curious to see what the snag forest was originally. Open large spruce and old hemlock with understory of tall grasses and devil's club. Heavy moss mats grow on the lower branches and scatter over the ground. Piles of cone bracts mark squirrel lunch spots at the ends of fallen logs. We work our way back through the tangle of fallen snags and drainage channels to the beach. By the time we get to the bank of the Nuka River, the tide is rising rapidly and forcing us into the snag forest. We establish another plot in the sparse sedges and start back. The tide pushes us further and further into the tangle of deadfall and channels. Areas we easily waded earlier are flooded now. Icy logs span the deep channels, and we teeter across these wearing hip boots and carrying equipment. Other drainages force long detours to beat the incoming tide. Finally we get out into open beach again, and Randy comes to pick us up. High overcast clouds move in as we wait for the fisheries and water crew to finish up their sampling.

The quiet of the bay is broken by a distant plane, and the Beaver reappears from the east. This time I talk directly to Paul Haertel, the National Park Service Associate Regional Director for Resources. I have been requested for Valdez duty by the Secretary of Interior's office in Washington, and there is no appeal. A Harbor Air plane will pick me up in an hour. I feel resigned as I pass on our schedule for the day so they can find me and go below to pack my gear. The work on the coast was nice while it lasted. Eric moves the *Shaman* over into Surprise Bay. A float plane can pick me up at the beach there.

As we pass into the inner lagoon of the bay, the rocks inside the entrance are visible at the base of the avalanche path. Palisade Lagoon is another beautiful spot. A narrow entrance between soaring bedrock walls opens up into a sheltered lagoon and small valley. Avalanches pour off the valley sides, replaced in summer with dancing waterfalls. Babcock Creek drains the main valley, striving to flow to the ocean, but falling short in dry weather and sinking into its gravel bed. In earlier years, this valley was the site of a busy gold mine. Now one man owns the lode claims and shares the valley with mountain goats, black bear and the occasional visitor.

We all row ashore and go our separate ways. Mike and I walk the full width of the valley to check out the vegetation types and set up a plot in the dense sedges near the mouth of Babcock Creek. I go a short way up the creek to check the stream gauge we put in last summer. It's still in place; only the top sticks out of the snow. The fisheries crew comes back from their survey. The stream is still frozen, and the snow is deep.

This is the valley where Bud's dog Sunny spent two winters on her own. Brought out to the coast as a pup by miners, she was left to fend for herself for six months each winter. Apparently she lived by feeding in the intertidal zone on mussels and winterkill. Maybe a goat caught in the avalanches. Local legend tells that she chased a black bear right up the side of the mountain and out of the valley. She'd get pretty skinny by spring when the miners would return and feed her for the summer again. Last fall the park boat brought her into Seward, and she came to live with Bud. She's a loving and independent dog and an excellent mouser, stalking and pouncing like a fox. She is still amazed that the food bowl is filled every day.

After we go back to the *Shaman*, Sandy sets up a water quality station just outside the entrance to Palisade Lagoon. I keep an ear cocked to the sky, but no plane appears. By the time Sandy finishes his sampling, the plane is four hours late, and I decide to proceed with our work rather than wait any longer. The delay of the plane is normal for communications and logistics in the back country, and I am both annoyed and relieved with the silent skies. We will be back in Seward tomorrow, and that will be soon enough to go to Valdez.

We have heard radio reports of oil moving west along the outer coast, so we make a run across lower Nuka Bay to the Pye Islands to check. There are about a hundred sea lions on the rookeries at the end of the Pye Islands. Although we stop several times to check, we don't find any conclusive evidence of oil. Sandy collects water samples at several points along the coast en route to Harris Bay.

The clouds get thicker and lower, and by the time we anchor outside the moraine in Northwestern Lagoon, a steady drizzle is falling. The black sand beach is very steep here, and Eric anchors the *Shaman* close to shore. Large windrows of logs and debris indicate a stormy coast, and Eric decides to go ashore for the first time for a little beachcombing. On shore I follow the beach around to the north, across the old terminal moraine and into the inner shore of the lagoon. The tide is about mid-high and rising, and the moraine looks like a barnacle and kelp moonscape of black boulders in the mist. Grounded icebergs have drug their feet in the sand and loom out of the coming darkness like ghosts.

A veritable lacework of land otter tracks is woven along the shore and down to the water's edge. The incoming tide nibbles the tracks away one by one to clean the slate for the next night's frolic. In bizarre counterpoint to kelp and otter tracks, huge colorful tangles of rope, net, plastic bottles and floats are enmeshed with the debris logs and morainal rocks. Here we find the first winterkill: three long-dead bird carcasses. Mike throws them over the storm tide line so they will not be confused with oiled carcasses later. This sampling and preparation for oncoming oil seems surreal in the cold half light, ringed by lowering clouds and mountain feet and grey water.

As I come back around the beach corner, I see Eric making a frantic dash for the skiff. Apparently *Shaman* drug her anchor on the incoming tide and Randy has called him back. We all reassemble on the beach, and Randy ferries us back to *Shaman* as Eric gets things squared away. As the weather is calm, Eric grants my request to spend the night in Taz Basin, a place I have heard about from friends, but have never seen. We arrive at the narrow entrance in the last light and pass through the opening in the rocks into a perfect teacup basin carved out of solid granite. The sides are vertical and high, and the floor of the basin is deep and smooth. After dark a swell coming in from the southwest makes Eric nervous, so he moves *Shaman* to the other side of the cove and re-anchors. One dragging anchor a day is enough.

We wrap up the day's notes and fix supper in the cozy warmness of the cabin. Eric puts on a tape and oldies make a gentle background for ordinary chores at the end of another long day. After supper I go on deck for awhile. All dark and misty except squares on the water from cabin window lights. We are encircled by rock walls, and a hundred waterfalls fill the chamber with echoes of falling water. The evening is quiet and peaceful, and I miss sharing this time with Bud.

One of the things that didn't get fixed in the frantic dewinterization of the *Shaman* was the pump to flush the heads. We solve the problem by pouring in buckets of seawater. As I tend to this chore in the dark, I notice whirling points of light in the bottom of the bowl. Delighted, I pour a couple more buckets down just to watch the phosphorescence. I've never actually seen marine phosphorescence before and I am enchanted. Going back on deck, I flail at the water's surface with an oar, stirring up a myriad of sparks and splashes. Imagine swimming in this in warm water! Wow! With a head full of fireworks images, I find my bunk and wriggle down into my sleeping bag.

April 5

We're up early in the grey light. From the pilot house, I watch the radar scope and rock walls as Eric maneuvers *Shaman* out of Taz Basin. Rocks close in almost to touching as the bottom rises to a lip on the fathometer. Then *Shaman* brushes over the kelp and out into the gentle swells on the west side of Granite Island. We cruise on down the island, around Granite Cape, and weave our way east through the islands to the Chiswells.

Here I encounter the oil slick first hand. After all the sampling and testing and wondering what it will be like, there is no doubt. The smell is nearly overpowering. The oil lays on the water surface as a blue-grey coverlet. The surface wind ruffling is dampened. At the edges, the thinner oil gleams in iridescent colors: yellows, blues, green, red. Thick brown globs float in the slick, the leading edge of obscene diarrhea from a sick monster. Only a few sea lions remain on the haulout rocks where we saw hundreds just three days ago. I finally spot about 50 swimming in the slick just off the rocks. Kittiwakes and gulls swirl overhead. Although the air resounds with gull screams and sea lion grunts, there seems to be a deathly stillness in the place.

Soberly, we go about the business of taking notes and collecting samples. Somehow we make the problem smaller by focusing on the scientific tasks. Oil is reduced when it is in a 125 ml jar. The globs are like heavy bearing grease, and

Randy only gets it off his hands after scrubbing vigorously with Simple Green cleaner. Silently, we leave this place and head northeast.

The oil coverage is in large patches. About one mile off Pilot Rock we encounter another wide band of oil and are still in it when we reach Barwell Island. Off the south side of Rugged Island we watch five whales spouting and swimming in the slick. It doesn't seem to quite touch the shore, holding just back of the line of breakers on the rocks. As we approach Barwell Island the oil is thick and stretches south as far as we can see.

Large flocks of kittiwakes and gulls wheel overhead, and kittiwakes and murres are rafted on the water in the oil. This is the beginning of migration arrival for many seabirds. Exhausted from the long flights, they raft up to rest and feed for awhile before beginning the arduous work of nesting and raising young. The rocky islands and headlands of this coast are some of the prime nesting habitat in the world for these species. In the weeks ahead, hundreds of thousands of birds will arrive to stay or pass through to other nesting areas. As they dive to feed and surface to raft with their companions, it is incomprehensible that they will not be contaminated sooner or later. External oil becomes internal toxins when the birds preen, trying to restore loft to sticky feathers. As the *Shaman* approaches the island we see birds with dark patches in white feathers.

The oil lies thick around Barwell Island, right up to the steep rock walls. The swells slosh gently forward and slurp back, continually washing the shore with oily water. The smell of petroleum is very strong, completely overpowering the normal sea smells of salt air and clean kelp. I ask Eric to go through the pass between Barwell Island and the cape. The oil has pooled here, an inch thick or more. We see more and more birds with oiled feathers, and I realize that we can't tell where oil ends and black feathers begin. Bobbing in the pass, we collect samples, take photos, notes. The rocks near the sea are sloping on the back side of the island. As I stand on the bow I notice movement in the dark rocks. Looking closer, I see a murre right at the water's edge, being washed by every breaking wave. She is completely black, her normal white breast feathers covered with oil. As each wave washes her anew with oil, she staggers to keep balance. Her wings flap feebly but don't generate any lift to fly. She tries to hop up the rock surface to escape the waves, but slides back down in the oil. The only part that seems to work is her tail, which she shakes vigorously after every wave.

As I stand alone on the bow, a deep grief begins to emerge in me. Beginning in my belly, it rises through my being and surfaces as sobs which shake my soul. The enormity of the horror washes over me, watching this lone bird beginning to die, struggling to live, in the stench of gasoline. The ecologist in me has known for days the destruction the oil is causing to entire ecosystems. Not just the death of individual animals, plants, plankton and lifestyles; but the total changes in the energy flow through the system. The dynamic flow of energy, nutrients and life is altered, blocked. The functioning chain of life, ebbing and flowing from one organism to another, from one generation to the next, no longer functions. The processes which flow through the land also flow through my being, and I feel the lurching, the recoiling, the aberrations in the smoothly functioning system. Tears overflow and course down my face, dropping onto the deck at my feet. A commotion at the stern brushes forward. "A bird, a dead bird." Someone rushes up to me: "Should we get it? Do we need it for a specimen?" Mutely I nod my head and stumble into the pilot house. Eric sees my tears and holds me tightly. "No need to apologize," he says, "I feel the same way." Gradually my sobs subside and settle over my heart like a heavy wet blanket. Quietly, *Shaman* powers up again and we head up Resurrection Bay. The oil only goes up the bay a short ways, and soon we are out of it.

We swing into Thumb Cove. Bright orange curtain boom is stretched across the creek mouth. It stands tall and garish against the tree and mountain pattern reflected in the calm sea. The people of Seward have not waited for EXXON to bring equipment and supplies to protect their salmon fisheries. Calls in the night and old contacts bring a planeload of scarce boom, and it is deployed by local boats just ahead of the oil coming across the Gulf. As we head on into Seward, the pesky Beaver flies overhead once again. This time it is Bud on the radio. We ought to each make it to the dock at the same time. "I love you" I venture onto the radio, for all the boat traffic to hear. Suddenly I feel bruised and overwhelmed, and I long for a little quiet time with him.

The dock is crowded as Eric berths *Shaman*. Anne Castellina, the Superintendent of the park, meets me with a big hug, and our closeknit crew is inundated by park people and press. I don't see Bud among them, so I go inside to gather gear. I am the last of the scientists off, loaded down with my equipment, and most of the people have dispersed. A lone photographer catches me as I come wearily down the dock. Up at the park office, people and questions swirl about in confusion. We bring the first oil samples from outside Prince William Sound. During the four days we were gone, an army of people has descended on Seward, focused on the park and the information we bring back.

I am hungry and tired and dirty. My heart has been raked raw by what I have seen and heard and smelled. I look forward to a shower, some lunch, telling Bud about my adventures. Instead I am catapulted into noise and demands. Something about investigators and interviews and evidence and intelligence gathering. Have they developed a new language while we were gone? Somehow I find Bud and after awhile, we escape to a restaurant for lunch, but we are interrupted several times by people who need to talk to Bud.

Fed, but not nourished, we return to the office. The ICT has grown by leaps and bounds and moved to larger quarters. Our crew is sent there to talk to the Park Service legal investigators. We go over what we have seen in excruciating detail. They don't understand our scientific language any better than I understand their legal jargon, and the interviews take a long time. Our samples and photos and notes become specimens, all with numbers, and have to be carefully accounted for and kept under lock and key. I want a cup of tea and a shower--instead we run all over town trying to find lockable freezer space. It is after dark when I finally hand over my soil and vegetation samples.

I am told to head for Anchorage and then on to Valdez as soon as I have finished the interview. The Regional Office people support my going to Valdez and tell me to speak the truth of what I have seen. After this trip to the coast, I know I cannot remain silent in the face of pointed questions from the press. Several phone calls later, I get off the hook. The investigators need a report from me and feel that much of the trip would be wasted if it's not written. A final call is made to the Department of Interior coordinator. He can't wait another day while I write my report. He tells me I'm blowing a big chance for "exposure" that would be good for my career. Where I come from, you die of exposure. I appreciate the opportunity, but suggest he contact Howard Levine, a colleague from the Bureau of Land Management, to go in my place. Later I call Howard, and he is glad to go.

Wearily, I drive to Bud's apartment. I have barely seen him since we returned, and there has been no quiet time at all. I finally step into the shower and feel the soothing hot water run down my body. Supper is sporadic when Bud gets home, as multiple phone calls interrupt. My own phone call to Anchorage is disturbing. Dad tells me Mom is in the hospital, recovering from hip replacement surgery. I hadn't even known the surgery was scheduled, and it took place while I was out on the boat. When I talk to Mom she sounds tired and in pain. I am numb when we go to bed, and Bud and I curl up around each other to sleep.

April 6

I surface slowly from sleep, realizing that Bud's arms are around me. Sleeping together is still a luxury for us. Our choices in careers and geography make our time together sparse and precious. As yet we have little sense of ordinary time, days stacked on days, finding our routines and patterns. But this is not ordinary time, and too soon we get up.

Early to the park office, then down to the ICT headquarters. My main objective for the day is to get a good start on my report. A web of counter demands pulls me this way and that: time reports, chain of custody forms, film processing, oil descriptions, lost gear, data base for tracking samples, returning the radios, maps, politics, updates and meetings. In addition to the report, I am asked to write up a procedures manual for the vegetation work. While we were gone, two other parks, Katmai and Lake Clark, are beginning to assemble people for their own pre-oil assessments.

The need to write the report keeps nagging me, and there is nowhere to sit down in the ICT headquarters, much less to work. I leave the noise and go back to the park office, hoping to find a computer and some quiet. I settle down at Bud's Compaq and try to gather my thoughts. I stumble through by fits and starts, between constant interruptions. After awhile Bud needs the computer, then I can't get anything out of the printer. Whenever I receive or make a phone call, I wander through the building trying to find a phone that doesn't have a body in front of it. Lunchtime comes and goes; I grab a tub of yogurt and drink too much coffee because it's the only hot thing available.

I suggest to Peter Fitzmaurice, the Chief Ranger for the park, that all of us working on the oil spill need to take time to rest and care for ourselves. I am feeling rushed and tired, and Bud has snapped at me and others. Peter orders Bud and I to take the afternoon off and recommends skiing in the sunshine.

We're scheduled to leave at 1:00; it's 3:00 when we finally get underway. We drive out to the bridge over the Resurrection River to ski into Exit Glacier. The day is warm and sunny, and it feels wonderful to get out of town. Sunny is staying with Anne, and we picked her up on the way. The snow is very soft and punchy. The river is murmuring softly through the ice, and the glacier beckons blue and crystal at the end of the road. Sunny is getting round from lack of exercise like the rest of us, and it feels good to be moving freely again. Bud's disposition improves immediately. He's whistling and cheerful within a half a mile. Mine takes longer to improve, but the sunshine and exercise lift my spirits, even if my ski poles keep punching through. Within an hour, Bud gets nervous about getting back to a meeting, and we turn around before we get to the glacier. On the drive back down the valley, we talk about how to support each other in this madness. Bud says it would be a help to him if I would put together a project plan for future work to monitor the impacts of the oil on the coastal environment. But first I have to finish my last report and write up instructions for other ecologists in Katmai and Lake Clark.

It is late afternoon when I get back to my report at the park office. As I try to think through the impacts of the oil on the system and the pathways it will take, I realize I don't know a whole lot about petroleum chemistry. I finally call Ed, my neighborhood petroleum engineer, and he gives me a quick lesson. More than I ever wanted to know about crude oil. Crude oil is composed of a wide variety of carbon compounds, from C_3 through C_{18} and larger. The "light ends," which evaporate easily, are volatile compounds composed of gases hexane, propane, butane, pentane, methane, ethane and others. When crude oil is put into the pipeline at Prudhoe Bay, additional "LPG's" or liquid petroleum gases, are added. This increases the percentage of volatile gases from a normal level of 10-20%, up to 25 or 30%. These light gases are evaporating and account for the strong gasoline fumes I have encountered when I am around the spill. The remainder of the crude is composed of diesel fuels, oils, light tars, heavy tars and asphalts. The sheen that is so noticeable on the water is predominately diesel fuel. The floating blobs are tars. The cold Gulf waters and specific gravity of some of these tars will cause the masses of oil to sink below the surface of the water, especially as the tar becomes mixed with silt and sand. Ed reviews a typical distillation report; boiling points and volumes of the various components. He adds a couple notes at the end about North Slope crude in particular: it has a higher sulphur content than crude from other parts of the world. And apparently dispersants don't work well on Alaskan crudes. I asked him how the oil company employees are reacting to the oil spill. He tells me of shame, disgust, anger and a feeling of broken trust in management.

I review the list of substances which have been released into this pristine system with revulsion. When I'm out in the backcountry, I take elaborate precautions for "minimum impact" camping, so that little or no trace will remain of my passing. But I also remember that many of the products that make my journeys in this land possible are petroleum derivatives: polypropylene, nylon, plastics, fiberglass, Kevelar, white gas, aviation fuel. It feels easy to assign the blame for this tragedy on Big Oil, or on the captain of the *EXXON Valdez* in particular. But at some basic level I'm beginning to realize that this disaster belongs to me too.

When I get home to Bud's apartment, I shuffle through the stack of mail and find the applications for the 1989 Permanent Fund Dividend. This is a program which pays an annual dividend from investments of state oil money to qualified Alaskan residents. With a sense of irony I fill it out and send it off before turning in at the end of another long and exhausting day.

April 7

The ICT holds briefings every day at 8:00 A.M. and 6:00 P.M. in their headquarters. Every morning all of us involved in the spill work assemble, sleepy-eyed and still fatigued, to review the day's work. After a hour-long meeting I make my way back to the park office and my report. It is relatively peaceful, and I finish a rough draft by late morning. As I'm working on it, Paul Haertel stops by. He is flying the aerial bird and marine mammal survey, and they need another observer for the afternoon flight. I'm drafted for the job, even though I'm not a good identifier of birds from the air.

After lunch our crew of four assembles at the airport. Paul is our pilot, Janet the recorder, and Dale and I are the primary observers. For overwater flights, we have to wear fire-retardant Nomex flight suits lined with floatation. We all look like hot doughchildren as we waddle across the asphalt apron. We're using an amphibious Beaver for the flight. As I climb onto the floats and open the door, the smell of it reverts me to childhood and flying with Dad. It's been a long time since I've crawled into a Beaver. As a child, I would be lifted up and seatbuckled down in front of an amazing bank of gauges and dials and levers. Then into the air on an adventure: new country, new people, sometimes even Anchorage, the Big City. No wonder that as adults all four of us children turned to aviation, either as recreation or a vocation.

We take off into the south wind and fly down Resurrection Bay. Another sunny blue day with brisk winds. Not good for oil movement down the park coast. Off the end of Aialik Cape we see whale spouts. Swinging over them, I can see their huge light bodies in the water. Moving up and down, blue grey when submerged, light grey hump when surfacing, and a steam cloud spout. The grey whale migration is moving through right along the coast of the Kenai Peninsula, following the nearshore current that is their highway. The current path is slightly warmer than surrounding waters. It moves east to west, swinging up through Granite Passage and then along the outer coast west of Harris Bay. Unfortunately, this current also carries the oil along the coast. We see huge patches and sheets of sheen and mousse all along the coast as far as Nuka Bay. The whales are surfacing right in it.

As we fly west, Dale and Paul give me a quick lesson in seabird and waterfowl identification. Dad would be a lot better at this than me. The water is brilliant blue and green near shore as we swing up Port Dick. The morainal shoals look like coral lagoons, and I comment that it looks like Tahiti. Janet, across from me, says it depends on where you're looking. Her window is filled with steep snowy mountainsides, glaciers and spruce forest. What an amazing country.

I see goat trails wound around the high country and bear tracks just above timberline. We cross over the logged area and through the pass to Seldovia and Kachemak Bay.

Here we start the survey, Dale and I calling out species and numbers of birds and animals as Paul flies about 200 feet above the sea. Different species of birds have different patterns of flying and congregating. Scoters, murrelets, pintails, cormorants, gulls, kittiwakes, eagles, goldeneyes, geese and "unidentified." Some flocks wheel en masse, others fly in a line, skipping just above the water's surface. Gulls wheel in disorganized circles, each bird for itself. Near the Fox River, newly arrived Canada geese rest on the mud flats and take short flights when the shadow of the Beaver passes over. Eagles ignore us, slowly flapping along the shore on their own errands. Sea otters look wonderful. From my vertical view they seem to be suspended in the translucent water, diving and rolling.

We fly all the way around the head of Kachemak Bay and back down the north shore to Homer. Here we land to refuel, then survey north to Anchor Point. A dark layer of clouds hangs over the mountains across Cook Inlet to the west, but Mount Redoubt and Mount Iliamna shine in the sun in front of the clouds. Late in the afternoon we head back along the outer coast to Seward. En route we map the oil offshore of the park. The leading edge of the slick is moving through, patchy sheen and stringers of mixed oil and water we call mousse. It stretches offshore into the Gulf, further than we can see, twenty miles or more. Paul flies me up each of the bays on the outer coast: Black, Thunder, Two Arm and the outstanding Northwestern Lagoon. I see some places we should consider adding to the vegetation work, maybe other disciplines as well. We fly on into Seward, landing in early evening. The oil mapping update is taken to the ICT, and it is late again when I get home.

April 8-9

We arrive at the ICT headquarters for the morning briefing and find the halls are swarming with people. The Park Service staff and the ICT are beginning to swell with incoming people. Now there are three offices filled with people, set up to handle the pre-oil assessment activities. Over fifty people are working on the oil spill in Seward, supporting about a dozen scientists in the field.

My Anchorage roommate Frankie Barker and a friend Glenna drive down to check in on us and get some firsthand information about the oil spill. I don't have much chance to talk with them, but give Frankie extra oil samples I brought in from the outer coast and an overview I have written. She is a co-director of the Alaska Natural History Association, which publishes and distributes books about Alaskan resources. Already she is beginning work on a book about the oil spill for release this summer. Saturday evening, Frankie and Glenna cook supper, and Bud and I come home to prepared dinner and welcome company. It feels wonderfully nurturing to have the apartment warm and full of food smells and to eat vegetables and salad and fish at our own table.

On Sunday Frankie and Glenna ski out to Exit Glacier, and Bud and I join them for a couple hours. As we approach the face of the glacier in the sun, we hear faint rumbles and a shower of ice shards starts to sift down. The ice fall increases over several minutes, and groaning and cracking, a large pillar leans out from the face and topples over right in front of us. A cloud of ice dust and snow sifts up over the new blue ice chunks. In the ringing silence, we ski on around the snout of the glacier, seeing other evidence of its activity in the winter: more recent ice fall, pushed up ice and bulldozed snow. Underneath some ice ledges ribbons of ice have formed from melt water. Glenna and I approach the glacier to explore recent activity. This makes our companions nervous, so we make our way back out to them on the outwash plain. Too soon we head back, work calling and the snow is getting soft.

Later in the day, Bud and I sit down with the State Parks man, Jack Sinclair, and the Fish and Wildlife seabird man to develop and prioritize a list of areas for protection from oil. We use Bud's map and our cumulative field experience to prepare a further list of critical areas. Sea lion haulouts, sea otter concentrations, sea bird rookeries, eagle nests, lagoon estuaries and recreational beaches. This is a rich and varied land, and the listing of jewels grows longer and longer.

It is very apparent to us that the highest priority is keeping oil off the shorelines by booms or skimming. Once oil hits the beaches and cliffs, major cleanup will be required. In late March Bud developed a list of critical and high priority salmon spawning streams and other high value habitats. This list of streams and lagoons is still the highest priority for protection. Finally enough boom is coming into Seward so that most of the spawning streams will have at least one cordon of boom around their mouths. I remember the triple strands I saw ringing the hatchery at Sawmill Bay and wonder how these single boom lines will be adequate protection.

April 10

My head is awhirl with concepts for evaluating the effects of the oil spill on the outer coast of the park. What to watch, what components to monitor, how to integrate the information to tell us about the functioning whole. The outer coast is remote and rugged, and until a few days ago, was pristine. The jagged coastline is a diverse mosaic of steep cliff headlands, sheltered shallow lagoons, long sandy beaches and glaciers pouring into the sea at the ends of long fjords. It is difficult to know where or how the oil will come ashore in the park, even more difficult to track the impacts to the land

and its occupants. Exposed bedrock cliffs will receive the first onslaught of oiling but will also "self clean" from the direct assault of storm waves. Upbay, the sheltered, low energy coves and beaches will be oiled more slowly, but the oil will be trapped in the soft sediments. Gravel on some beaches is turned over, and the crashing waves will stir oiled rocks deep into the beach.

I unplug and steal Bud's computer, taking it up to the park conference room hoping to find a little quiet workspace. I make a list of the critical components as an outline and start writing. By the end of the day, I feel drained, but I have an eight-page draft of the oil spill monitoring plan. The amount of work I have outlined seems daunting, but I think it is achievable without costing an outrageous fortune, and it will give us an idea of the type and magnitude of impacts.

The first critical element is to track the progress of the oil, mapping the extent and intensity of oil contact. We have to collect samples of the oil itself, as well as the waters and beaches. Survey the beaches for oil strikes, oiled carcasses and general condition. As on-shore cleanup activities get going, we will need to monitor their progress and effectiveness, as well as evaluate the balance of damage versus the benefits of the cleanup. In addition to direct effects of the oil itself, the natural systems will need to be monitored to assess the impacts of oil in the environment--seabirds, marine mammals, bears, wolverines, land and sea otters, eagles and other scavengers, plankton, in-stream fisheries, intertidal plants and animals, and terrestrial vegetation. Then the harder questions of how this effort will affect human use, the sites of prehistoric occupation and current recreational activities.

The plan has a few questions and blank spots, smart-ass comments from when I got real tired, and it hasn't been through the spell checker. But it is important that we get some kind of overview plan so Bud can send out the next round of scientists. This effort makes for a very long day, and once again it's 8:00 before Bud and I leave the offices. Today oil has been reported on actual park shores for the first time, and Anne has urged us to increase our effort to monitor the progress and protect whatever is possible in the park. I'm glad she smiles as she tells us this; I am already completely immersed in the oil spill work. Although I'm maintaining equilibrium, I have no reserves of energy to throw into the fray.

April 11

I spend most of this day refining the monitoring plan. I develop a large chart for each study, showing expertise needed, names, dates and timing, logistics and equipment. The spelling gets corrected, the comment about bears and cheese sandwiches stays in. Late in the afternoon I hear from the National Park Service Regional Office in Anchorage. It appears that my draft plan has been widely distributed. This is certainly premature, but all I get is "It's a good plan, keep working on it." I feel uneasy about some parts of it since they are outside my immediate expertise, but there are no major corrections. I've given Bud a copy for review and ask to talk it over with him. I feel that he can give me the most comprehensive feedback, especially about the details pertaining to this park.

It seems that there is literally no time for Bud and I to simply talk to each other. Every day is long and complex. We eat in restaurants where we are constantly interrupted throughout the meal by ICT members or other people who need to talk with Bud. We barely make it home at night in time to go to bed, and too early we have to get up and go again. I still haven't been able to talk with Bud about my boat trip into the fjords. I finally give up on finding time to talk about personal experiences, but I do need to talk with him on professional issues. So does everybody else. After a few days, I specifically ask him to have lunch at home so we can go over the study plan for a couple hours without interruption. There is a meeting at 2:00, so this is the only time available, and I can't proceed on the plan without input from him. But just as we are leaving, Bud decides to move an old computer out of his office. We spend 45 minutes unplugging components and carrying them up to storage. When we get into the car to leave, half our time is gone. I dissolve into tears.

After a lifetime of silence, I have finally learned that one way to get through hard times and to enjoy joyful times, is to talk with other people about what is going on. It helps to clarify how I feel about events, helps me to learn what they mean to me, helps me to release the pain and move on. I have gradually come to have a wonderful network of people whom I can turn to, and Bud has become an integral part of this network over the past year. Here in Seward, I am away from the rest of my network, and I start to put heavy expectations on him for support. But there is no time for talking through any personal feelings, and now it feels like there isn't even time for talking about our work. As the days go on, I try to find other people in Seward to talk with, to get a hug from, to somehow make a human connection. But everywhere I turn, everyone is enmeshed in the frenzy, focused on the crisis of the instant.

The other vital part of my sanity maintenance is quiet time to be outdoors, often while hiking or skiing. Bud and I have shared many hours in the mountains or ski trails, moving together in silence. Often physically apart, but aware of a bond between us. There have been magic moments on the Coastal Trail in Anchorage, two lycra-clad bodies wafting through the trees in the setting sun, pausing for a kiss in the face of Denali, a quick hug by new moose tracks, gliding on with the wind in our hair. These activities have fallen by the wayside from the start of the oil spill. The few short moments we do have are wrenched from the demands of the system, grabbed in spite of the pressure.

Unaware, I start to accumulate the confusion within me, frantically moving through the days in a cloud of work to keep my heart above the rising level of pain. Bud and I start to drift apart, the connection of the past year and the wedding slowly being submerged by the turmoil surging around us.

April 12

Spring and the oil continue to arrive concurrently in the land. Geese and ducks start to appear on the small lagoon near the park headquarters. The population of Seward swells to nearly double normal numbers. Quiet streets are streaming traffic at all hours. Often it slows to a crawl as ducks waddle across the highway. The sun shines bright, but cold brisk winds continue to push the oil along the coast.

The boats of the fishing fleet are beached near the small boat harbor. As I walk through them, the sound of hammers, country western radio and shouts echo among the gleaming hulls. Another spring ritual, as old as humans who fish in this land: the preparation of boats and gear for herring, halibut, cod and salmon. Children play giggling hide and seek among the cradles and propellers. Occasionally a request is shouted down to hand up tools, or climb up on deck and lend a hand. As yet EXXON has not availed themselves of the boats and expertise available in the fishing fleet, causing anger and raised voices in villages around the spill. And already the herring fishery for this year has been cancelled in Prince William Sound. Oil and herring roe both coated the kelp in shallow waters, and fishing families sit by as large portions of their annual income is lost. The rest of the fishing season is totally unknown: Where will the oil go? How long will it stay? Will it sink to the ocean floor and contaminate halibut? Will it be suspended somewhere in the water column and foul gear? Will it lay in the gravel near spawning streams and poison returning salmon, and kill the growing fry? Will we lose this entire age class of fish, and have a dearth every three or four years? For now all these questions remain unanswered, and despite their anger, commercial fishers continue to prepare for fishing, because this is spring, and in spring you get ready.

All around me I see and hear the approach of the coming season. We have had a light snow pack this winter, and by mid-afternoon each day, it has warmed up and is isothermal and rotten. Mud and puddles pit the roads. The streams flow around old ice. When I pause I hear sounds of water from all directions, my ears separating the threads of flow or absorbing the whole tapestry of running, falling, dripping meltwater. The first robin sings, I find pussy willows high in the branches. A early golden dandelion gleams from a crack near the foundation of the bank. Then the first cautious unfurling of willow leaves, the rich smell of sap rising in the cottonwoods, the daily delay of sunset behind the mountains.

And throughout each day, the litany of oil progress along the shore: streamers of mousse wound around the Chiswells; patches of tar near Cloudy Cape; huge sheens reaching through McArthur Pass, into Nuka Bay, stretching offshore beyond the aerial surveys. There is a map-covered wall in the ICT headquarters, and each day it is updated with aerial observations. The oil distribution is mercurial, pushed and pulled by wind and tide and seas. In the briefing each evening, I hold my breath as the story of fouling unfolds. Sometimes a beach is free for another day, surrounded by darkened waters. Then another jewel is reported with oil on the shores.

I remember the pristine coast I was privileged to kayak last summer with Bud, the wildness where Mom and Dad took us as children on our tiny *Sailboat*, where we ran free along the beaches. Gleaming white ice walls of glaciers pushing into the ocean, pale grey misty days softening the outlines of jagged rocky shores, strong winds and scary waves tossing our little boat like a fleck of foam. The tangled pattern of shells and seaweeds and otter tracks. But new images are superimposed on those sparkling memories: the black tide lines I saw on Knight Island, the vast oil slick stretching to the horizon, the gooey greasy tar balls floating in lower Resurrection Bay. I think of the Dr. Seuss story of the Cat in the Hat that Mom read to us during winter nights in front of the fire. In the story, the dirty bathtub ring grows and spreads from its bathtub container throughout the house, over the floor and furniture. All the efforts of the Cat in the Hat only extend it more, until it is completely out of control and covers his universe. In the end, he brings in the assistance of many small cats and a little magic, gets it corralled again, and cleans it up. But this is not a fairy story, it is a nightmare, brought on by arrogance and complacency, and there is no magic to bring a happy ending.

The Incident Commander starts to talk about pulling the ICT out in a week or so and turning the operation over to EXXON and the Coast Guard. This would be appropriate in the normal course of events, but as yet we have seen no evidence that either entity is ready to assume the workload. Reports from Valdez are full of confusion and conflict, politics running rampant between government agencies, and very little results on the waters and beaches of the Sound. One night there are new faces under western hats, presumably from EXXON, but they have nothing to say.

Anne assembles the core of the park staff at her house for pizza and planning. At the end of the evening and a bottle of wine, we have designed a workable organization to continue the oil spill effort. One major side of it is the post-oiling damage assessment and evaluation, a task I can assume if I choose to. This would allow me to stay in Seward for the summer and provide a challenging opportunity to implement the monitoring plan I have written.

It is near midnight when Bud and I get home, our heads awhirl with the plans of the evening. We drink tea and read to calm down before going to bed. In sleepy comments Bud expresses concern with having both of us so intimately involved in this work--myself as the science coordinator and him running the operations side of the coast work and serving as resources advisor. It seems that we are to have too much or too little of being together. After planning to live in separate cities with weekends together, we have been living with each other for our entire marriage except three days. The possibility of a whole summer together looks good to me, even if stressful conditions prevail. We go to bed without resolving anything, but Bud's concerns give me sober thoughts and shadows of similar situations in a previous relationship.

April 13

By late morning, several of the top managers from the Anchorage Regional Office come to Seward. Anne reviews the table of organization and responsibilities from our session the previous evening, and it is approved. I am appointed the Injury Assessment Coordinator for the Kenai Fjords National Park. It is my job to design and implement the scientific work which will provide data on the impacts of oil on the park and near-park lands, complete some of the work myself, monitor progress of the oil, work with EXXON and the other agencies on cleanup activities, and integrate all of this into an understandable whole. I will coordinate the scientists that will study and document the effects of the oil spill on the park and collect samples and data to support claims against EXXON for damages. We will set up the Injury Assessment Center in a building across the street from the park office for this work. I decide to gradually build up the staff, finding expertise for specific studies as necessary. One valuable position which I will start with is an assistant. Barely three weeks into the oil spill and I am hopelessly behind in everything, from phone calls to photo labeling to laundry. Already I feel my concentration slipping and my effectiveness deteriorating.

I have much to learn about the assessment process of resource damage as outlined by CERCLA, the Comprehensive Environmental Rehabilitation, Compensation and Liability Act. It takes us several days to even get a complete copy of the legislation and regulations in Seward. The Park Service has imported an expert on CERCLA and the Clean

Water Act to guide our work. This is to ensure that we will have the data and samples needed to support federal claims, and that we do work that is covered under the regulations for reimbursement. CERCLA defines a precise set of steps to be taken to determine if and how much damage has been done to the environment and the resources of the public. This procedure will control the work from here on out. The final result is that a dollar value is placed on the damage. Financial settlements are to reimburse costs incurred during the assessment and quantification of the damage and for the actual financial value to restore or replace the damaged resources.

My planning becomes confined by tight but ill-defined boundaries. CERCLA only applies to natural resources, so assessment and damage to cultural resources such as old pit houses or stone implements is not included. In the preassessment phase, samples can only be collected; the actual laboratory analysis of the samples is not authorized for anything that will keep. Water samples have to be processed within 72 hours, but soils samples are frozen for later work. It is necessary to "confirm the exposure" and determine the impact, but a regular monitoring schedule is not allowed. I struggle through these new concepts and terms, attempting to get definitions solid enough to define our work for the summer. The assessment phase is supposed to evaluate the type and quantify the injury for damages. But by the time they go through the process of selecting the Authorized Official, set up the complex organization of Trustees, prepare an assessment plan, hold the 30-day public review, and then start to implement the plan, it will be fall. And the oil is washing down our shores by the hour, and already the cleanup politics are becoming complex and full of differences.

Accepting the position of Injury Assessment Coordinator means I will remain in Seward and work on the oil spill for the summer. Although the job is scarcely calm and stress free, the monitoring plan I have laid out will give me focus. I have run other projects this complex and know what it takes to build a team that can focus and function in a high stress, goal-oriented environment. Take responsibility for yourself, look out for the other guy, recognize and value the contributions of each member. Although the chaos swirls around me, I feel that I will be able to take care of myself, to find the support and nurturing I will need to survive the months ahead. Besides, it appears to be the only way I will see Bud all summer.

April 14-15

The next few days are reasonably quiet, if long. Bud is out on a four-day trip to the coast with Anne and the head investigator to confirm the presence of oil on park shores and collect samples. I spend long hours working on the schedule for the summer's work, listing and ordering equipment and supplies, coordinating with scientists in other agencies and the Regional Office in Anchorage. The emergency nature of the situation allows different rules for hiring and purchasing than generally used by the government. I hire Mike Tetreau to work with me for a month until he resumes his regular job of trail building at Exit Glacier.

Following the schedule of the monitoring plan, I start laying out objectives, crews and logistics for several more trips to the outer coast. We need another trip to monitor seabirds and marine mammals as the oil front moves along the coast. Then another longer voyage to do in-depth mapping of oil contact on park lands. The details of the trips overwhelm me. There is an intense controversy about containers for collecting oiled specimens. Apparently we need special jars which are only manufactured by one place every other Tuesday, except this month and last month. Usually they supply laboratories and the order for the oil spill completely swamped their plant. The alternative is to use glass jars, but they have to go through about five washes, starting with a dishwasher, distilled water, and something else. I'm asking people in Anchorage to order and prepare these. After a long series of yeah--buts, I'm at the end of my rope when a man says he can't do it because there isn't a dishwasher in the Regional Office. Then someone wants an archeologist to go on the oil mapping trip. Find an expert in intertidal environments who is available. Locate and get a team ready for another seabird and marine mammal survey to go out as soon as Bud and Anne return on the *Snowbird*.

April 16

Late in the morning, a radio message is relayed that the *Snowbird* is inbound for Seward and should arrive in an hour. A boat washing station has been set up by the Army dock in the small boat harbor for vessels that have been out in the oil. In the driving rain, I wander around the back roads of the railroad yards and docks until I find the ramp to the Army dock. As the *Snowbird* slowly approaches, the boom is opened, then closed behind her, and she's made fast to the dock. Bud seems weary, but excited; this is the first voyage he's had to the outer coast since this started. He acts distant, no hug, no kiss, barest of eye contact. The deck of the *Snowbird* is covered with tarps, and these are marked with dark bootprints. The white hull is caked in dark brown tar at the waterline. Marks of slapping waves in the slick. A white plastic bucket on deck is brim full with thick foul tar and slushy snow. The smell of petroleum permeates the air as we unload the boat and lug the gear up the docks to the trucks.

All four of the crew are cumbersome in bright orange Mustang floatation suits. These too, are streaked with tar. They have come back from another world. Their words shape images like fractured shards of glass: scraping oil mousse off rocks with a paint scraper as the waves lurch the Avon against the cliff; a beach of granite boulders white on top, black and gooey beneath; oiled logs in the strandline; bird carcasses thrown in the rocks by storm surf.

Steam and detergent curl around the hull as the *Snowbird* is cleaned. The boom holds the surface scum, but what happens to the dissolved oil and detergent washing into the waters of the small boat harbor? The white bucket of mousse is set aside on the dock, a vile symbol of the whole event. We step carefully around it so we don't tip it over into the small boat harbor. No one knows what to do with it, where to throw it away. Five gallons out of 11 million . . .

The crew has several hours of work ahead of them before showers and rest can even be considered. The specimens are cataloged and stored, interviews given, reports to the ICT briefing, updating everyone who grabs their sleeves in the street. Another late night before Bud and I are home. Bud has the flu and crawls woozily through the shower and into bed. He is in shock but not surprised by the extent of the oiling. At some level he is vindicated by the oil's path, following his forecast the day he first heard of the spill. But this is no comfort when seeing miles of tarry sheen in Nuka Bay, his summer station for four years.

April 17-18

We start into another work week without a pause. More and more people pour into Seward, trailing along behind the oil front. The Coast Guard quietly sets up shop in the ICT headquarters to coordinate the oil spill recovery and cleanup. The National Weather Service comes with computers, and we have the luxury of local and current weather forecasts. The team of investigators expands to handle the massive volumes of data and evidence we're collecting. Other agencies send people who pass through for a day or two, but few stay to help. They all want to talk with us, get the latest update, hop a lift out to the coast if possible, then move on.

Seward begins to feel like Fairbanks during the early days of the pipeline construction boom. Some very strange people are walking the streets. One afternoon as I am returning from an errand to the small boat harbor, two men step out of a local restaurant in front of me. I am verbally assaulted, and they literally grab at me, forcing me to step off the sidewalk. We have two separate incidents of theft and vandalism at the Exit Glacier Visitor's Center, the first since the Center opened seven years ago. One night new menus are placed in front of us at a local restaurant; all the prices are raised by one to two dollars. Seward is starting to cash in on the oil spill boom.

Somewhere in this timeframe, the east coast of Katmai National Park gets creamed by the oil slick. Three hundred miles from the origin of the spill, and the oil is still spreading. Nancy Deschu, a hydrologist friend, was on the outer Katmai coast as the oil arrived. She tells me later of walking sparkling clean beaches one afternoon, knowing that the oil will come on the night tide. And the next day, she is put ashore alone to walk the beaches all day, recording and sampling the thick tar which covers the rocks, leaving lumpy bird carcasses in the mousse. She tells of perching on a big boulder, trying to find some clean place to set down her camera so she can write notes. Of walking ankle deep in the oil, sliming her boots and raingear.

VECO is the company that is the subcontractor to EXXON for the oil spill cleanup. I hear that VECO's contract calls for cost reimbursement of expenses plus 10%. It doesn't take an economic genius to figure out that their objective is to spend money, which is different from cleaning up oil. Wild stories circulate: VECO people walking into the local hardware store and dropping $20,000 on garbage cans and shovels. Inflatable boats and Mustang floatation suits are now unavailable through the nation, all bought up by VECO.

A bright spot in this time is a letter handed to me by Anne. Written by Anne Hoover-Miller, she expresses concern for the land and offers to help. Bud tells me that she did research on harbor seals in Aialik Bay, and she usually lives with her husband in Day Harbor, between Resurrection Bay and Prince William Sound. When I call her, she sounds competent and sane, and I ask her to fill the Technical Coordinator position to work with me. In addition to her scientific expertise in marine mammals and sea birds, she can handle a boat, knows the country and weather, can design and set up projects, and as a wonderful bonus, is a computer whiz! She can arrive about May 15, which coincides with Mike resuming his trail job.

April 19

In the first days of the spill, the National Park Service was one of the few agencies taking the threat of oil off the coast of the Kenai Peninsula seriously. Other agencies focused on the immediate disaster in Prince William Sound with an appalling lack of concern to the threat of oil outside of the Sound. People were still in shock that it actually got out of the tanker in the first place. It seems that they simply could not believe that the oil would spread so far.

Now the agencies are beginning to realize that the oil spill is no longer contained within the Sound, and additional people begin to appear, hopefully to stay. Many of them don't realize that some work has already begun or that the ICT is in place. The Fish and Wildlife Service has several people in town. Their primary work centers on bird surveys, and collecting, identifying and cataloguing the dead birds and animals that are brought in. It is nasty smelly work, standing under a tarp in the wind-driven rain with sacks full of disintegrating bird carcasses. The Alaska Department of Environmental Conservation (ADEC) has brought a helicopter and several people to conduct daily mapping of the oil progress on the shorelines and offshore. The National Oceanic and Atmospheric Administration (NOAA) has arrived to coordinate the scientific activities.

While I was out on the *Shaman* in early April, a Multi-Agency Committee (MAC) was formed in Seward to help advise and guide the work of monitoring, containment, and cleanup. The MAC is open to all groups who are involved with the oil spill, and right now it is composed of local representatives of a few agencies, the City of Seward and local businesspeople. Anne, the Park Superintendent, is the chair of the MAC. The MAC can advise the Coast Guard but has little actual authority to act.

After talking to individual agencies for a couple days, I suggest to Anne that the scientific people ought to meet to coordinate the projects so we don't overlap or leave out pieces. Through the MAC, she sets up a meeting time and place for scientists. The initial purpose is to exchange information about projects, coordinate logistics and people, try to make data compatible so we can integrate it later, and keep abreast of the work on the outer coast.

The first Resources MAC meeting is informative. Six or eight of us gather in the park's small conference room. We exchange information on our work and coordinate logistics. We don't elect or appoint a leader as it doesn't seem necessary, just a round robin of information exchange. It almost seems like a restful pause in the frantic days, to sit still for an hour or two with no phones. I had figured these meetings would be held once or twice a week. But when we set our next meeting time, the man from NOAA wants daily meetings like they have in Valdez. So we agree to meet the next day at 7:00 P.M. With the ICT briefings, this makes three meetings a day.

April 20

The myriad of details avalanches over me. All requests for people, equipment, and logistics are submitted to the ICT on a written form, where they get logged and filled. This includes every little detail--a form regardless of whether I'm ordering felt tip pens or a vessel for a week. When I get the hang of it, forms fly and I carry a supply at all times.

I continue preparing for the voyage to go out and map oil strike on the shorelines the following week. We will use the *Spirit*, the cruiser that Kenai Fjords Tours uses for their Aialik Bay tours. I line up a crew of six or seven people, and outline the tasks we need to accomplish: mapping extent of oil on shorelines; inventorying dead birds and animals and arranging for their removal; collecting samples of oil, water, plankton, fish and soil.

In the midst of all this activity, I still have no place to work. I try to base out of the park office because there are literally no empty chairs at the ICT headquarters downtown. I have put in phone requests several times, but the Seward phone company is completely overwhelmed. I use a brown manila folder for a desk. Critical equipment, papers, computer files, specimens, photos and negatives are all moved and misplaced several times daily. I literally do not have a square foot of space where I can put my stuff and find it there when I return. At home things are similar. Bud's home is so small that there is no room for my gear. I pile duffel sacks outside his door or heap stuff in the back of my car.

Bud and I find we are about to become land barons. Bud has been considering the purchase of a house in Seward for nearly a year now. The sale becomes final in the thick of the oil spill work. And we have the opportunity to purchase the Manitoba Mountain ski cabin we have been borrowing for the winter. These are both dreams coming true, but the paperwork realities are time consuming and confusing. Repeatedly we have to go to the bank to review and sign loan papers, then insurance, see a lawyer about the cabin, Forest Service permits, Borough taxes, insurance again. I refuse to sign a carte blanche Power of Attorney over to Bud, and this causes consternation at the bank, until we edit it to deal with the house. Being married changes our legal status, but not my name, and the system is not set up to deal with our choices. Half the paperwork is written in for somebody called Mrs. Rice, and all of it has to be corrected and redone.

Our second Resource MAC meeting lasts two and a half hours. New people are present, and much of yesterday's material is repeated. Our lack of an elected leader seems to bother some, and the leadership is arbitrarily assumed by a few domineering people. When we stumble home at 9:30, neither Bud nor I have eaten since noon, and the choice of cooking or sleeping is difficult.

April 21

I finally request that someone send my phone number rolodex and calendar from my office in Anchorage. I suddenly realize that it is the time of full moon, and Bud and I have been married a month. Before the wedding, I had reserved Forest Service cabins for a group of us to go into Juneau Lake and spend these four days skiing and exploring the mountains. We've been on skis twice since our honeymoon; usually we ski daily all winter. Now I can't even find the receipt to cancel our reservations.

The work of the oil mapping trip preparation continues. I ask Steve Hackett, an outfitter and friend, to go with us. He wants to get to the outer coast, would be a big help with the work, and could assist with planning and buying food. Sandy will go again, but he has to find an assistant. Shelly may or may not go, depending on whether EXXON starts a sea otter rescue center in Seward. At the Resources MAC meeting, I ask the State to send someone, and the Alaska Department of Fish and Game promises a representative.

One of the major concerns Bud brought back from his trip to the coast is the presence of oil soaked carcasses washed up on the beaches. He watched eagles and other scavengers feeding on the bodies in the tidelines. This scavenging moves the oil and toxins onto the land and up the food chain. Soon bears will be out of hibernation and patrolling the beaches for winterkill. It will look like a bonanza. Somehow we need to get the carrion off the beaches. The bird rescue boats have been bringing in some carcasses, but they are concentrating on live birds and get their dead birds off the water. The Fish and Wildlife Service is cataloguing and storing all carcasses, and they don't want birds removed or destroyed without records. We spend a lot of time trying to find solutions to the bureaucratic restrictions and the practical realities of piles of rotting ducks. Black humor abounds as we discuss ways of burning them, and Bud spends a couple hours in the wind-driven rain with a torch, determining that only the feathers will burn, and only with difficulty. We finally work out a solution with Fish and Wildlife such that if we will identify the remains and collect location data for them, we will not have to be the ones to return the actual birds. We decide to ask VECO to assign a bird boat to follow after us and pick up the carcasses after we have located and identified them. VECO is amenable and asks us to coordinate with the Bird Rescue Center for a vessel. This evening, the meeting runs to 8:30, an improvement, but I am getting more and more tired every day.

April 22

Bud and I decide to take tomorrow off and go skiing and to go to our cabin at Manitoba Mountain for a couple nights. Tonight I simply say I have another appointment and leave the Resources MAC meeting at 8:00 P.M.

I have the apartment to myself for a half hour or so until the meeting ends and Bud comes home. It is very quiet. Both dogs are farmed out; my dog Misty is still in Anchorage, and Sunny is staying with Anne until Bud gets his new house. I sit on the couch in the silence, holding a cup of tea, trying to relax. My brain whirls with details, but I can't seem to focus or let go. I should be up packing food and equipment so we can leave for the cabin. More and more, I'm starting to feel split; part of me is like a dervish; another part is detached and watching. When Bud returns, we drag stuff out to the car and load skis. Bud's friends, Kim and Charlie, have asked to ski with us, and they will join us at Turnagain Pass tomorrow. When we get to the cabin about 10:00, the trail is drifted shut, and the walls are full of cold. We start the fire and tumble into bed.

April 23

Bud and I wake to a cold grey subdawn. The fire is long gone in the stove, and we snuggle together to preserve the only pocket of warmth in the cabin. Finally thoughts of hot chocolate and skiing lure us out of sleeping bags, and we hustle into clothes and start the fire. The balloons from the wedding reception are still in the corner, withered like shed skins of celebration. The flowers from my hair lie frozen on the table, dry brown orchids contrasting with the dull sparkle of the rhinestones.

Groggily, we go through morning rituals, almost forgotten in the past frantic weeks. Wood fire crackling in the stove, heat radiating in an expanding circle to encompass the big chairs, but never reaching the corners of the cabin. Propane stove for hot water, big boots to push through the snow to the outhouse. Laden with packs and skis, we stumble down our narrow path through the moose tracks to the car.

Wet sticky snow begins as we drive to Turnagain Pass, and we arrive at the summit as rain and snow swirl around the windows. It looks foul, perfect weather for hypothermia or spending the day by a fire. When Kim and Charlie arrive, we all have to talk ourselves into trying it. Raingear would be more appropriate than lycra. But my inertia falls away as I clip into heavy skis with climbing skins and start up the first slope. Through the rain and slush, I follow familiar paths, places I've skied since I was a child. We climb smoothly up the open slopes, past the soft, snow-piled hemlocks that always look like ghosts, secret trails through the forested groves, up the narrow draw, to the highest patch of trees on the mountain. The wind comes and rain becomes sleet, thrown against us in stinging sheets. We pause for shelter in the last hemlocks, grab a handful of gorp and a swig of water.

By the time we pull the skins off our skis for the descent, fingers are turning numb and we are becoming chilled. We turn downward, thrashing through the breakable crust. Awkward traverses and kick turns, marked by great craters where we fall. We start laughing at each other, then giggling at ourselves. The snow is horrible, and we are cold and creaky on skis. As we move down into the trees again and thrash about in the drifts, we warm up, and the snow improves. Soon we're even making two or three turns in a row, cheering each other on for every flailing curve, howling at every fall. After awhile Bud and Charlie get ahead, and Kim and I stand in the quiet of the hemlocks with snow drifting down. We talk and laugh and talk some more. I am hungry for the connection and the laughter, the soft whiteness gently caressing my face and piling on my hair. I lose track of time, standing surrounded by snow ghosts. As of old, I take my ski pole and give some of them grinning faces. Finally we hear calls from below; Bud and Charlie are concerned that we are lost or injured. They are put out because they have climbed back up the hill without skins looking for us. I can't even feel properly apologetic. How can I get lost here? And I've climbed these hills hundreds of times without skins with no permanent damage. The snow gets heavier as we savor the last few turns, then make the long traverse back to the parking lot.

At the car, a complete change of dry clothes feels wonderful. This small break to a clean and snowy mountain is refreshing, the first cooling breeze on my soul seared by too much work, fatigue, and the submerged pain from a darkened coast. Both body and heart feel nurtured as Bud and I head north to Anchorage.

I went to Seward for a week and have been there three already. I need to get more gear, grab bills, see my mother. At the hospital, Mom seems in good spirits but laughingly tells of passing out in physical therapy. It is a shock for me. She looks smaller, surrounded by machines and white sheets. She asks about our work, but I can hardly find words. Bud does better, carrying much of the visit. In this small pause from the job, other realities start to hit me, including my mother's vulnerability. I look at the flowers around the room and remember I haven't brought any. Only a daughter in slow motion.

Afterwards, Bud drives through puddled Anchorage streets up to my home. Misty greets us enthusiastically. It feels strange walking through the house. Frankie's Christmas kitten Taz has grown, items have been moved, there are new issues of magazines and piles of newspapers with oil spill headlines. I gather some more polypropylene, hip boots, my medication, the stack of mail, all the film I can find. I feel like a stranger here, as though I'm moving through the house in a soap bubble. I try to talk to Frankie and Patty, but feel unconnected. Too soon we load the car, call Misty to join us and head back to the madness. Another night at the cabin is welcome, but we're in Seward the next day before the 8:00 A.M. briefing.

April 24

The last of the first ICT is pulling out, and the transition to a smaller team is in progress. The full work load of the ICT drops on six or eight people, in addition to their regular park duties. I claim a small desk in the mail room and move my equipment there. Still no phone, but at least I can pile papers and think they'll stay in place. Preparations for the oil mapping voyage accelerate. Mike shows up and is an incredible help in dealing with logistics. The issue of dinghies raises its head once more. I refuse to go with *Tin Lizzy* again. Mike goes into the warehouse and ransacks through the park inflatables to find one that is complete and doesn't leak. Steve Hackett calls and says he won't be able to make the trip. I repeat my request to the ICT to have food planned and purchased for the trip by one of their people. They suggest to me that I call Job Service and get a high school student to do the food.

Right--food for nine people, ten days. I have visions of Twinkies and frozen pizza for a week. Anne pulls Bud from the trip because she doesn't want both of her main resource people gone at the same time. I am now one person short of the minimum I need. I am disappointed because I had looked forward to sharing this work with Bud and being out on the coast together again. Besides, we desperately need his skills, and he is not easy to replace. Sandy has found an assistant and will be here with help and complete equipment. Bless him. I start searching frantically for a replacement for Bud, someone who can identify birds. Fish and Wildlife has two possibilities, but one has a new baby and the other has field work. I spend hours on the phone chasing one dead end after another. By the time I get home this evening, the trip is falling apart faster than I can put my thumbs in the leaks.

April 25

I am on the road by 6:00 A.M, returning to Anchorage. I need to talk to my boss, Alex Carter, and this morning is the only time we can get together. When I get to the Regional Office, it is quiet. Our entire Branch is gone, working on the oil spill from the Wrangells to Katmai. Alex and I escape the office and sit drinking tea and talking. He has no idea when his staff will be back, as many of us have key roles in the oil spill effort. It looks like I will be gone the entire summer, thus forfeiting all the field work I had planned for my regular job. Alex had been looking forward to this summer and fall to get down to work on our main job in the Region, the actual management of mining activities. But he returned from a trip to Denver in early April to a row of empty offices and a staff scattered on boats and beaches.

I spend the lunch hour scurrying around town doing errands. My mail box is crammed, and I put in a change of address form to Seward. I stop by Keller's Photo Lab and drop off negatives and an order for wedding photos. My wonderful sparkly silk wedding dress goes to the cleaners. I handle it gingerly, my roughened fingers catching in the delicate fabric. Barely a month ago, over a lifetime ago, I was a bride. Candlelight and balloons and solemn words and joyous music. Now it feels like a fairy tale told to me at bedtime.

Back at the office, I meet with people who have reviewed the monitoring plan I wrote. Repeatedly I am told "Just go do it, Page." I get the message; I tell Paul that if he wants me to stop or change it, he'll have to pull my chain. Otherwise, we're in business. Late in the afternoon, Assistant Regional Director for Operations, Dave Ames, calls me into his office and asks if there is anything he can do to help. I ask for a seabird expert to go with us on the voyage. He picks up the phone, talks to Chuck Gilbert in the Lands office, and arranges for him to join us. What a relief--back to full crew again. It's short notice for Chuck, but he is game. He did the seabird survey of the outer coast five years ago, so he knows the waters and the birds.

When I left Seward last night, there was still no arrangement for purchase of food for this trip, and no one I've asked is willing to assume the task. I don't want to face a week-long trip with no grub. I become like the Little Red Hen in the children's story and decide to do it myself. I have no list, no quantities, no menus. I do know we have a refrigerator, freezer and oven on board the *Spirit*. At the wholesale supermarket, I wheel a large cart up and down the aisles, grabbing packages and stacking them high. Nine people, seven days, plus three days of emergency supplies. I hope none of the crew are vegetarians or have weird allergies. The only request I have heard is for snack food. Fruit, bread, cheese, muffins, butter, meat, potatoes, granola, juices, etc, etc, etc. Towards the end, the cart is piled high and a five-pound bag of Gummi bears tops the heap. The groceries barely fit into my Subaru. I swing by to see my sister Lynn for an hour or so before heading home. It is after 10:00 when I get to the house, and I can't face another two and a half hours on the road tonight. I sleep in my own bed for the first time in a month.

April 26

Another early start, but the drive back to Seward is quiet and beautiful. The sky lightens as I drive up Turnagain Arm, and the sun touches the mountaintops through Turnagain Pass and up toward Summit. I make a brief stop at the cabin to pick up some gear. The quiet and peace of the snow drift over me. A chickadee welcomes me from a birch branch. I want to rest awhile, start the fire and drink tea, don my skis and climb up to the rosy sun, listen to Fresno Creek gurgle to itself under the ice by the bridge. I savor the clean white snow and crisp cold air and the solitude. For an instant I forget I'm already on the treadmill for the day. I'm pretty much running on automatic pilot these days, shifting between places, people and tasks without much emotional involvement. But even a plane on automatic pilot makes continual minor adjustments to stay on course, and these tiny moments of peace and beauty are my course corrections. Perhaps never before have I noticed and savored such small respites, minute joys, flashes of wonder. Then the noise of a passing truck on the highway gearing down for the curve breaks my serenity, and reluctantly I head back down our narrow trail. As I drive down the last canyon to Seward I can feel the miasma of crisis and franticness and pain close over me.

Bud is already at work when I reach the park office. I find him long enough for a morning hug and am rewarded by a look of pain. All the park staff have had to wear their full dress uniforms, including ties, since the oil spill began. For reasons I can't comprehend, the tie tack is backed by a sharp point that hits the wearer in the middle of the sternum. I keep forgetting this feature, and poor Bud has a bruise on his chest. The system has a uniform that doesn't even allow hugs without pain. What is the message here? We move the tie aside, and I hug him gently again. Even as we try to have a few quiet words together, swarms of people are tugging at us for attention, pelting us with questions and demands. The cabin quiet melts from my soul, and we each turn to face the myriad of details.

When I check on the radios I requested two weeks ago, I am told they are on order and won't be here for another six weeks. We cannot do this trip without radio communication between the shore teams and the boat. Firmly, I tell them that we need radios and to borrow some from BLM or the Forest Service or someone.

I need to empty my car and get the groceries settled in appropriate refrigeration. Fortunately, the new building for the Injury Assessment Center across the street is nearly ready, and it has freezer and cooler space. The small Injury Assessment staff hopes to move in before I am back from this voyage. As I carry boxes of groceries, someone runs alongside me--"How many phones, how many lines, how much furniture, where do we get it . . . ?" I have barely thought about any of this. Standing in the middle of the empty space with a box of oranges in my hands and a loaf of bread nudging my chin, I try to envision the working space. I give them an outline of phones, furniture and dividers.

Lunchtime swirls by. I snatch yogurt and a candy bar out of the trip food. I realize that I haven't had a real meal for a day and a half. Later I go over to the Kenai Fjords Tour office to finalize plans for tomorrow with Pam and Don Oldow, the owners/skippers of the *Spirit*. The calm of their office and ways are gentling to me in the madness. Pam gives me a hug before I leave. Hugs are becoming a real premium item for me. There is little to no personal contact among the people working on the oil spill--no hugs, no touching, no eye contact, no caring words. I treasure every one I can find.

On the previous day, two people from Human Affairs of Alaska came down to talk to the park people about how to cope with stress in the disaster environment. I missed the meeting because I was in Anchorage but make an appointment for my own session over the phone. After an hour's talk,

I go home, unwilling to face the Resources MAC meeting. It is so nice to get to the quiet of Bud's home, perched on a hill above a creek. I spend a few minutes in the porch swing listening to the breakup murmurings of creek and runoff and watching Misty play. It's good to have her in Seward, gentle big fluffball dog, patiently waiting for hours, always glad to see us come home. An early eagle circles the valley and settles on an old cottonwood across the creek.

Swinging slowly, I reflect over my conversation with the counselor. She explained that this is not like a natural disaster, which is usually part of a natural cycle with a definite end and which we can more easily accept. The oil spill is an unnatural event, caused by human complacency and error. She says we are having normal reactions to an abnormal event.

These past few days, I'm starting to feel worn down, unable to concentrate or focus. My brain is beginning to go fuzzy, and I keep losing or forgetting things. Bud and I have pretty much become disconnected from each other, whirling in our own little spheres, brushing together for the briefest contacts through the days. The counselor told me to define my basic requirements for physical and emotional well being and to make a plan and set limits to provide these minimal necessities. For the upcoming boat trip, she suggests real basics: take some favorite tea, get a trashy novel to read, try to get some sleep, concentrate only on the job at hand.

Too soon I have to leave the quiet summer evening and pack my gear for the trip. Early spring can still be a cold and nasty season on the coast, and my duffel bag bulges with heavy raingear and several changes of polypropylene everything. I find a book and slip in one of our wedding pictures as a bookmarker.

Bud gets home about 9:00, and tells me that the State man who was going on the trip has just been pulled off. Damn! One short again. My brain races through people who have offered to help, but this is very short notice. I call a friend in Anchorage, Karen Jettmar, in the hopes she is available for a spur of the moment adventure. Karen is a professional photographer and we could make good use of her skills. She is just getting home, and I wait while she parks her bicycle. "Hi Karen, do you want to do a trip to the outer coast tomorrow? Boat leaves at 10:00 A.M, bring your cameras." She only makes a slight pause before rearranging her schedule. She can make it to Seward on the first flight in the morning. Another adrenaline rush subsides, and wearily Bud and I make some supper and crawl into bed.

April 27

We struggle awake in the bare dawn light, and I stumble into my last shower for a week. Arriving at the park office, we hit the deck running. Low tide is about 9:00, so it will be difficult to get the *Spirit* to the loading ramp. We may need to delay departure a little, which will give us a couple badly needed hours. Radios have been located, as if by magic, and will arrive with Karen on the morning flight from Anchorage. I find someone to go pick up both. Checking in with VECO with a map and schedule of our trip, I am told that we still do not have a bird boat to follow us and gather up dead birds. I accompany the VECO man to the Bird Rescue Center to arrange a contact boat out in Nuka Bay. Although we are there over a half an hour, the woman who is running it literally will not talk with us. In disgust we leave, and VECO hires another boat, the *Jessi Girl*, to assist us. We will meet them in two days in Nuka Bay. By this time, the tide is coming in, and Don has brought the *Spirit* around for loading.

The dock is a beehive of activity. Our crew swarms over the *Spirit* with loads of equipment and food. EXXON has finally located absorbent boom, and it is piled up on the ramp like white cordwood. The Fish and Wildlife Service is preparing a trip out with the *Foxy Lady* for sea otter rescue work. On top of the pile of their bags and boxes are the large blue dog travel cages for transporting sea otters from the outer coast back to Seward. We load the park vehicles and shuttle back and forth like army ants, carrying loads to the *Spirit*, tending to last minute errands. In the midst of the frenzy, a new shift of investigators shows up and want to spend an hour with the entire crew. They get ten minutes on the end of the ramp, while Don and Randy are loading inflatables. Finally all gear is on board, if not stowed. Anne and Bud stand in the cold grey drizzle on the dock as we cast off. I linger on the bow as the engines gently push us out from the pilings and the strip of water widens between us. Carefully, Don turns the *Spirit* around in the narrow space by the gas float, and we motor out of the small boat harbor between low grey skies and calm dark water. There are a lot more people and activity than when we cast off on our first voyage a month ago. Several float planes are tied up in the harbor, and small boats are scurrying about all over Resurrection Bay.

We all busy ourselves with organizing and stowing gear and food as the *Spirit* heads south past the buoys and leaves Seward astern. We are eight on board; Don Oldow is skipper, Randy our deckhand again. I am crew lead for this trip, working with Mike Tetreau on the task of locating and mapping the oil on the park shores. Sandy Milner heads up the water and fisheries research again, assisted by Jeff Brownlee. Karen Jettmar and Chuck Gilbert have the unenviable task of counting and identifying bird carcasses on the beaches, so they can be collected and removed.

The *Spirit* feels like a luxurious vessel. In normal life, she is the tour boat for the Kenai Fjords Tours, carrying hundreds of visitors to Aialik Bay to see wildlife, birds and glaciers. Sixty-three feet long, twin engines, a full bank of radios and electronic navigation gear. In a squeeze, there are bunks for twenty. However, with all our equipment and two inflatables, outboard engines, fuel and foul weather gear, there is little extra room. The galley is amazing: running hot and cold water, microwave oven, full refrigerator and a freezer below decks. Three staterooms and a showered bathroom are tucked in the bow. Randy bunks in the lower hold, and I opt for the other bunk with him. We are quickly dubbed the bilge rats.

The surface of Resurrection Bay buzzes with boats zipping around and aircraft overhead. Otherwise the country seems normal and contrasts with the expectations for our work on this trip. Sea otters float serenely, bald eagles flap slowly along the coast or roost in tall spruce. Don alerts us to the passing sights while we work, just as though we were on tour ourselves. We pass close by the cliffs where mountain goats perch near the waterline. There is only a slight swell in the seas as we round Callisto Head and head for Bear Glacier Beach.

The whim of the winds has pushed oil sheen and mousse in and out of lower Resurrection Bay. Sometimes it holds off; sometimes it comes ashore. I imagine a misbehaving monster in the head of each fjord, sucking in water and squirting it back out, moving the oil up and back along the shores. It's a deadly game of roulette for the beaches, birds and bears.

I go up to the pilot house as the *Spirit* parallels the long steep beach in front of Bear Glacier. Bear Glacier is the widest ice tongue flowing off the Harding Ice Field. Although the glacier face has not been at the ocean for a long time, the end of the glacier was stable on its terminal moraine for several hundred years, dumping till and building a beach nearly five miles long. The glacier is currently receding, melting back faster than it flows forward, but still a very impressive sheet of fractured ice, especially on a sunny day. Even on a calm day, the surf is high and heavy on the cobble beach. Although we are very close to the shoreline, I cannot discern oil on the rocks. ADEC landed here in a helicopter in the past day or two and reported oil and dead birds along the length of the beach.

A lone aluminum skiff from the "mosquito fleet," a swarm of small skiffs hired by VECO for a variety of jobs, patrols slowly offshore, dragging a small loop of absorbent boom. The two men seem cold and bored, slumped down in the skiff to stay out of the wind. There is no visible oil on the water here. A common complaint heard around Seward is that there is no specific direction for the work of the mosquito fleet. As a result, much effort is expended in clean waters, and oiled waters often go untended.

The *Spirit* turns south at the west end of Bear Glacier Beach and we check the little coves along the west side of the bay. Bulldog, Porcupine, Agnes and Pony Coves slip by as the clouds get dark and lower, and the wind picks up. A barge is tucked into the back corner of Agnes Cove to collect large logs and debris, and hopefully to take on mousse and water collected by skimmers. So far the skimmers have had very little success, which may be just as well. There is very little barge space to empty them, no place on shore to store the oil and debris, and no good plan for disposing of the waste.

The slick from the oil spill extends over 600 miles from upper Prince William Sound, down through Montague Straits, along the lower coast of the entire Kenai Peninsula, over into Shelikof Straits, and down along the coasts of Kodiak Island and the Alaska Peninsula. Tar has been reported on the beaches in lower Cook Inlet nearly 300 miles from Bligh Reef. The slick has plastered the shores of Katmai and is reaching for Aniakchak National Monument and Preserve.

Cleanup efforts flounder in logistics and the magnitude of the task. In Prince William Sound a variety of techniques have been tried. Hoses strung along the oiled beaches continually spray low pressure cold water, trying to wash the oil off the rocks into the water where it can be caught inside booms and removed by skimmers. Another method involves high pressure fire hoses with hot water, hoping to blast the oil off, again into the ocean for skimming. Various chemicals are applied in test areas, searching for a miracle cleaner that will make all traces of oil disappear. And many people are on their knees in filthy raingear, literally picking up rocks one at a time, wiping off the loose oil and setting them down again. The beaches resemble a modern war zone crowded with people and technology. The trouble with all these methods is that each tide undoes the previous 12 hours work with a new layer of oil.

At sea the effort is focused on removing oil before it hits the shores. The oil spill caught everyone with a serious lack of materials, equipment and technology. Only a little boom was physically in Valdez. Stockpiles of boom within the state were minimal, and supplies of it throughout the nation were sparse. The City of Dutch Harbor in the Aleutians Islands, just recovering from its own recent oil spill, sent Seward several thousand feet of their boom supply, leaving themselves unprotected. Boom manufactures all over the world are operating at full speed 24 hours a day, and huge planeloads of it are finally showing up. Many kinds of boom are laced about the coast: fat white absorbent sausages called Hot Dogs, black and yellow barrier boom with a fringe of plastic in the water to stop oil movement, the huge two-meter wall boom from Norway. The theory is that the booms are drug through the slick by a pair of boats and the accumulated oil is pumped up by a skimmer.

But for many areas, it is too little, too late. In frustration, many people turn to native materials and ingenuity. Cordova commercial fishers use plastic buckets and flour scoops, bringing in more oil than EXXON skimmers. People in Homer and Seldovia use chain and logs with fringe absorbent to build booms. Seward commercial fishers use their boats to drag their nets through the slick to try to break it up. The emerging problem with all of these methods is the not insignificant issue of disposal after the oil is collected.

Stacy Studebaker, a friend and school teacher in Kodiak, conducted experiments with her class on oil spill cleanup methods. She used one half a quart of oil for the entire class, pouring it onto pans of water. The students used eyedroppers for skimmers and tested dispersants. At the end of the class, when they tried to clean up the lab, they found the "dispersed" oil was stuck hard to the bottom of the pans. And they were left with three huge garbage sacks packed full of greasy paper towels to clean one pint of oil.

Cormorants stand with outspread wings drying in the breeze on the rocks at the north end of Cheval Island. Gulls swirl around, moving white flecks among the black cormorant statues. We follow the west shore of Cheval Island south, bobbing in the swell scant yards off the rocks. Don saw mousse on the water in here two days previously. There is a wide black band around the rocks just above the waves. It sure looks like what we imagine oil to be on the rocks, but gulls are picking among the cracks and don't appear to have oil on their feathers. A seal surfaces alongside and peers curiously at us. No oil evident here, but we can't see very far from the deck. The wind is still picking up as we go past Pony Cove and squeak through the swells in Chicken Pass. Standing in the pilot house behind Don, I chuckle as I remember my only other trip on the *Spirit*. A couple years ago, I paid $70 for a tour and went where Don wanted to go. Now I'm being paid to do this work, and Don takes the *Spirit* where I want to go.

We encounter our first oil of this trip off Aialik Cape. It is a thick tangle of oily strands, kelp, sticks and flotsam in the offshore swells. It is different from the oil of a month ago. When it was new the oil was dark black along the shores of Knight Island and full of fumes from the evaporation of lighter components. On the previous trip it was spread out, the multicolored sheen of diesel with tar globs. Now a month later, it is mousse, a storm-beaten mixture of oil and seawater, reddish brown and very thick, full of debris, coiling around kelp and driftwood and shoreline like a boa constrictor. We don't stop for samples here as the seas are getting higher and the deck is too far above the water to reach without launching a dingy. Rounding Aialik Cape, I watch for the Dall porpoises which frequently join boats to frolic in the bow wave. But there are no approaching bursts of exhaled steam, no flash of white and black bodies beneath the hull. We cross lower Aialik Bay and thread our way among the lower islands and Pete's Pass. More mousse in the tide rips, but the weather is coming down, and I want to get all the way out to Nuka Bay tonight.

We go straight across the south end of Granite Cape and head for McArthur Pass. Smaller fishing boats headed for Seward are heavily bucking the waves. Even the *Spirit* rolls a little, and white caps start to build around us. All vessels in the area are supposed to check in with the Coast Guard cutter which is stationed in Nuka Bay. Although I try repeatedly to raise them, we never make contact. There is a lot of chatter on the radio, though few of the boats are in evidence. Listening to them, it sounds like our original destination, Moonlight Bay, is already crowded, and the weather report is full of building seas and winds. We raise the *Shaman*, which is serving as a medical boat now. Eric is anchored up in Surprise Bay, and Don decides to join him there.

The current is at slack tide as we enter McArthur Pass, so we miss the standing waves. Oil is evident on the tops of the rocks, and colorful sheen and brown scum cover the water. The longshore current pulls through this passage between mainland and the islands, and the oil river has been flowing through here for days. The whales we saw on the previous trip have migrated on to the summer Arctic. As we approach Harrington Point, there are several boats milling around just off the rocks. Each boat has a ring of filthy brown splatter marks smeared at the waterline. Don talks to one of them and learns that this is one of two localities on the outer coast where the marine telephone can be heard. So this is the communications center, and everyone bobs back and forth, waiting their turn for the line. EXXON has been working on radio communications for the coast, but as yet, there is nothing functional. The only communication is the marine radio system, which works well on the water but is poor for talking to town.

It is getting dark as we round the island at the entrance to Surprise Bay and work our way into the protected waters. The *Shaman* is the only boat there. The *Spirit* pulls alongside, and lines are made fast between the two vessels. The clouds lower below the mountain tops as we make supper and catch up on the news from the *Shaman*. Medical boats are on standby to be available for illness or injury of the people out on the cleanup. So far there has been little action, and they are getting very bored and are glad to see us. Don decides to spend the night rafted with the *Shaman* rather than wrestle with the *Spirit's* anchor. After supper we clean the galley and secure the lines. I am tired as I go down to my bilge bunk. Don has turned off the engines, so it is quiet, and the water slaps the hull beside my head. It has been another long day, and I am sound asleep before Randy turns off the light.

Sometime later, I awaken in the pitch black dark to feel the *Spirit* rocking. Muffled voices and footfalls on deck, the waves are more urgent at the waterline beside my ear. After awhile, the engines start, then shut down. Except for the waves, all becomes quiet and I sink into unconscious sleep. Then again, I am jerked out of sleep with loud banging right above my head. The wind is howling in the rigging and antennas, and waves are coursing along the hull. This time the footsteps are faster, up and down the deck above me, and voices shout above the wind. In the dark, I locate my clothes and go up to the main cabin. Don and Eric are working out in the rain, and I struggle into raingear and go out to help. The anchor has drug again, the engines start up and we move further out into the bay and re-anchor and re-secure the lines between *Spirit* and *Shaman*. It is incredibly black and the rain is sluicing down. In the anchor light's glow I see angry waves and white caps tossing around the hull. The shore is only visible on radar. Gusts of wind snarl around us, throwing rain against the boats. Neither Eric or Don took time for raingear and they are soaked, hair plastered to their heads. Finally the boats seem secure, and I head below again. This time I don't take my polypropylene off as I crawl into my sleeping bag. Randy is sleeping soundly. Later he tells me that he is deaf in one ear, and he sleeps with his good ear to the pillow. He never heard a thing. I drift into sleep with waves for a lullaby. And yet again, I am awakened by pounding footsteps, banging hulls, whistling wind. By the time I make it up to the cabin, we are loose from the *Shaman* and I see her anchor light off our bow across the bay. The anchor chain rattles out, the diesels throb as Don sets the anchor, then quiet falls in the dark.

April 28

This time I sleep through until Randy's watch peeps off at 6:30. I am the first up and a grey dismal morning greets me. Fog fills the bay and only a narrow line of green and black shore shows below the white curtain. Gusty winds scurry across the water, kicking up rough water and white caps. And the rain falls relentlessly. The *Shaman* is anchored to the south of us. We aren't going anywhere for awhile, and it's been a long night. I set the coffee to drip and savor a cup of hot chocolate in the solitude.

After awhile, the crew starts to straggle up with heavy eyes. Don gets his coffee, and I take a cup of tea up to the pilot house. Don invites me in and we watch the weather in silence, broken by occasional radio calls. It has been a hard night all around, and most boats are holed up for the day. Don tells me that the wind was so squirrelly last night that it got underneath the bumper buoys and blew them up above the railings of the *Spirit* and *Shaman*, then crashed the boats together. He sat up there on watch in the dark and realized that he owned both of these vessels that seemed intent on damaging themselves. The anchor on the *Shaman* drug three times, unable to hold both vessels in the 60-knot williwaw winds. We can barely see the shore now and aren't about to venture out in the small inflatables. Back in the cabin, we get a leisurely breakfast and work on notes and organizing gear. Mike feels under the weather and goes below to sleep.

Several hours later, the gusts dissipate a little and I decide to try a trip ashore. We are anchored off the Waterfield mining claim. No oil has been reported in Surprise Bay, but I decide to check the beach here for oil evidence.

On this trip we have all been provided with Mustang suits. These are large orange one-piece suits, two layers of nylon sandwiching neoprene. Reflective tape stripes the shoulders and hood, a blow-up tube inflates the collar. Wide webbing velcros cuffs, ankles, waist and thighs. They are sized big, bigger and biggest. I start with layers of polypropylene, then bunting and hip boots, and then struggle into the Mustang suit over it all. By the time I'm dressed, I'm hot and tired and can barely move in the bulky suit. The crotch hits me halfway to my knees. None of the webbing is tight enough to seal me into the suit. Bumbling about the deck, we manage to lower the small Avon, hand down engine, gas can, oars, and equipment. Mike, Chuck and I half climb, half fall into the Avon and head for shore. Fog is still down, rain falls in sheets. Gusts of wind scud across the water around us. Tide is inbound, and we drag the Avon up the beach and run out the anchor.

The beach is made up of shiny black broken slate, speckled with white and blue shells and strands of kelp. The three of us walk parallel lines around the length of the beach but find no evidence of oil. I dig down and collect a sample at the mid-tide line for later testing. We scramble up the washed out road to the mine entrance and peer into the tunnel, but it is dark and very wet. An abandoned ore cart stands on the track between the tunnel and the tram line, and electric wire and hoses are festooned around the rocks. From this perch, we can see out over the bay: low fog, two anchored boats and wind gusts scattering patches of white lace caps over the dark water surface. The short climb renders us sweating in the Mustang suits, despite the prime hypothermia weather. We waddle down to the beach and wrestle the Avon back into the water.

The wind continues to abate, so it appears safe enough to take the Avon up into Palisade Lagoon at the head of the bay. Sandy and Jeff are working on their water studies from the deck of the *Spirit*. As we approach the entrance to the lagoon, a line of brilliant yellow boom is stretched across the water. It seems to glow through the gloom and fog. Warily we approach, wondering how to get past it with the Avon. It is bolted together by sections and tied to exposed spruce roots at the water's edge. This is a barrier boom--inflated stuffed sausages of yellow plastic with a short curtain below them. It is intended to serve as a physical barrier to surface oil movement. Mike cuts the engine and tilts it up, while Chuck and I push down on the boom with the oars. As we struggle to slide the Avon over the boom, a sea otter peers at us from one side. An instant later she dives and surfaces on the other side, as if to demonstrate the proper technique of boom maneuvering. Silently, I implore her to stay in her hidden lagoon, away from the deadly oil on the outer coast. This boom has small gaps in it where oil can slip past, but if the oil gets here, perhaps the boom will keep some of it out of the lagoon. This is one of the fisheries that was on Bud's list, a small run of pink salmon spawns in the stream and intertidal waters at the head of the lagoon.

Once over the boom, Mike restarts the engine for the short run to the head of the lagoon. We see another otter, early ducks and cormorants. The wind is calmer on the water here, but tears away wisps of waterfalls which are plunging over the cliffs above us. On shore, we walk the beach at three levels, looking for evidence that oil may have come inside the lagoon. But all we find is kelp and soaked beach ryegrass and sedges bent over and winter pounded. I collect a soil sample from the vegetation plot, but there are no green shoots in evidence. Snow is still thick in the forest behind the shore. Babcock Creek is running open to the sea now from snowmelt and rain. We wade up the stream to read the rain gauge that Bud and I put in last summer. This combination of Mustang suit and hip boots isn't too bad, as long as we move slowly. Hands and face are the only exposed body parts. The benefit of the large suit becomes apparent as I pull my arms up inside the sleeves and hide my hands behind the cuffs. I am reminded of Farley Mowat's description in *People of the Deer* where the Eskimos have cold and windy tents for shelter, but sit warm and snug inside their individual tents of caribou skin suits. We reassemble at the Avon, reporting clean shores, scattered styrofoam, and no dead birds or animals and return to the *Spirit*.

Sandy has taken over half the cabin with his water quality analysis. He has brought equipment to do some of the analyses on-site to match the procedures used by other scientists in Prince William Sound. We fix a hot lunch while Sandy and Jeff finish up their work. It involves some very delicate measuring and balancing of fragile glassware on a makeshift cardboard stand. Chuck has brought a laptop computer, which he can run off the generator. Throughout the trip, whenever we come back to the boat, he sits down and writes up notes on the spot. We tease him about it, but it is an excellent record of the voyage. Mike is feeling very ill and crawls below into his bunk.

After lunch, the weather has settled down enough to make the run to Beauty Bay. Large swells are running in the open mouth of Beauty Bay, but they dissipate up near the beach at the head. Beauty Bay is one fjord in a complex of deep bays which make up Nuka Bay. It is shorter than most fjords, open toward the Gulf storms, with a wide valley at its head. Beauty Bay is unusual in that the valley behind it is glacier-free through the mountains, thus allowing migration of moose through the pass from Kachemak Bay to the outer coast. Like many of the fjords, the mountains rise without beaches from the ocean surface, with a few sheltered coves tucked into the rocks. We anchor off the south end of the long sweep of beach. Sandy and Jeff load up the large Zodiac for a full water quality, plankton and fisheries sampling regime. The head of the bay is very shallow, and it is easy to get caught by the tide here, so Randy ferries Karen, Chuck and myself ashore and will pick us up later when we radio him. We land on the steep rocky shore at the extreme south end of the beach and start walking three lines along the beach. The tide is about three quarters high, leaving 50 to 200 feet of exposed beach below last tide line. Rain is still falling steadily.

I walk with my head down against the rain, watching the beach at my feet. Wave-rounded pebbles make up the steep strand, with patches of shale outcrops. The fractured shale is composed of sharp vertical leaves of rock in the beach, like a book fallen on its back and soaked in the rain. In places we scramble over the rocks and fallen spruce. As I drop off a large trunk and splash through a small runoff creek, I am stopped by the sight of slight dull colors in the water. Looking closely, I see the tar balls on the beach. Dark brown black, they look like bittersweet chocolate melted into the rocks at the edge of the riffle in the stream. The colors come from light oily sheen leaching from the tar balls into the freshwater stream. Chuck and Karen join me. Looking around, we see more and more tar balls along the tide line. Apparently they came in on the tides in the last 24 hours, floating with the leading edge and grounding during the retreat. They are in two lines about a foot below the kelp line of recent high tides. They range in size from an inch to a foot across. Taking a rock, I scrape one. It is soft and has oozed down into the pebbles an inch or two. In the heavy rain, the water runs off the surface or balls up in the wrinkles. In the fractured slate, oil has penetrated into the cracks between the black leaves.

We begin the ritual of collecting and documenting a sample. For this trip, we have been given special sets of dual jars in a cardboard canister for the specimens. We are supposed to collect a sample in the jars with a trowel, assign it a unique item number, label the lids of the jars, then the canister. Then write all the pertinent information on a green card and photograph the entire collection. The system begins to fall apart immediately in the cold rain. The trowel is too big to slip oil into the mouth of the jar. The tar sticks to *everything*. We decide to take pebbles with the tar and scrape it off the trowel with more rocks. Then the tar gets onto the trowel handle, the jar lids, our hands, our suits, our boots. It adheres tenaciously, resisting removal even with the soggy paper towels I find in my pack. We finally get clean enough to write, but the marker won't write on the wet surfaces. The green cardboard card disintegrates as Chuck writes on it. Karen gets out the latest Olympus camera they sent with us for official photos. Her hands are still clean, as she has been busy taking pictures. Finally we get through the whole procedure and repack the equipment.

Shouldering our packs, we start off around the beach again. The tar balls are strung all along the tide lines. As we scramble over a bedrock outcrop, we find places where the tar balls were thrown against the rock by waves, sticking at the high water line and dripping down the rock faces, pooling in the crevices with kelp and shells. Further on, a lone white seagull feather is laid over a tar ball, raindrops beaded on the shimmering surface, smeared brown below where it touched the oil. The sandy beach in the southwest corner of the bay is clean of tarballs, raising our hopes that we have seen a freak hit of oil and the rest of the bay is clean. A large flock of sandhill cranes lowers out of the sky, calling in the grey wind like rusty hinges. They double back over the bay and settle in on a snowfree patch of tideline sedges. Chuck moves on ahead, while Karen and I carefully walk the debris lines. Now that our eyes have a search pattern, the oil is easy to spot by the beaded water, but the color is similar to the cobbles. This is a beach where I was with Bud last summer to install a stream gauge. It was warm and sunny then, the meadows back of the high tide full of wildflowers. Crows sat in the spruce branches and cackled at us and each other. But now I watch my feet carefully, images of tar balls in the pebbles swimming before my eyes, hoping against hope that it is a mirage.

As Karen and I linger over photos and otter tracks, we hear a shout from Chuck. More tar balls in the sand. He is on a shallow sand and mud beach formed from earthquake subsidence and alluvial outwash from several streams. The tar balls are thick and dense here. Large pancakes of mousse, two to three inches thick, one to three feet in diameter. They are scattered throughout the area in lines, looking as if a diarrhetic cow wandered the beach in confusion. The cranes mutter among themselves and lift off en masse, swirling against the mountain walls. The mousse pancakes reach inland nearly to the first vegetation plot, and I make another collection of oiled sand, for comparison with previous soil samples from the plot locations. An eagle watches us from the top of a spruce snag. We follow the mosaic of mousse east until we come to the banks of a large stream running out of the valley. Across the stream, the mousse patches continue. We cut back into the snag forest. Moose tracks weave between the dead trunks, and the fallen timbers are a jackstraw tangle to our progress. We move apart, each in our own thoughts, mobile orange stumps in the old grey snags. The cranes return with six tundra swans to land right in front of me. Their foraging grounds have been oiled, but they don't recognize the new element in their ancient patterns. Their long grey necks and legs rise and fall as they feed in the snowfree sedges. We watch in wonder from behind our tree trunks, privy to the spring patterns while recording the evidence of environmental outrage.

We have done our job in this place and with a sense of weariness I call Randy and ask him to come meet us on the beach. The water people are still hard at it; they have a long task at each station. Back on the boat, Don tells of radio calls he monitored. Just down the coast from Nuka Bay, Gore Point pushes a long sandy hook into the longshore current. This area is being heavily hit by oil, as the water-borne mousse, debris and dead creatures accumulate. The *Anna Lane* reported 600-700 dead birds washed ashore. Dead birds and animals are supposed to be collected and taken to Fish and Wildlife for storage. But the number exceeds any capability of the bird boats in the area. The crew attempts to identify and count the bodies, then burns them on the beach in an effort to keep eagles, otters and bears from feeding on the oiled carcasses. Later I hear that they are fired from oil spill work for this effort.

On board the *Spirit*, everything is very wet. We wash our boots and Mustang suits with a scrub brush and Simple Green as we step onto the deck and then take off the entire outer layer before entering the main cabin. Hip boots and orange suits are heaped over the equipment stored under the upper deck. Later Mike rigs a line to try to keep them out of the rain. Quietly, we organize our thoughts and notes. I have two sets of maps, and after every trip ashore I record the beaches walked and condition of each. Oil samples are stored, notes are written, film supplies refurbished. The fisheries crew comes back as we finish. Towing the Zodiac, we motor up the North Arm of Nuka Bay.

I go topside to my niche in the pilot house, watching the shoreline scroll off the bow with anticipation and dread. The North Arm is new territory to me, and each new cove and hidden rocky beach beckons for exploration. But having walked the oil line in Beauty Bay, I wonder how many of these strands and rocks are shedding water in greasy patches. I study the maps and aerial photos to select beaches for inspection. The large long beaches at the edges of big valleys are important for wildlife. Don swings in a small bay in the northwest corner of North Arm. High on the mountain walls above us, he points out a long slender white waterfall. It tumbles over 900 feet down the rock faces of the glacier-carved valley. The water launches over an alpine scarp, down over the subalpine of alder and hemlock, and crashes into the coastal conifers. During spring breakup or late summer glacier melting, the waterfall soars way out from the cliff, and rainbows flash in the mist.

Sandy, Karen and I go ashore on the long beach at the head of North Arm. The beach fronts a wide valley with a large river flowing silty and rampant through the floodplain. Seeing no evidence of oil on the beach, I follow the old flood channels upstream. The willows are high and thick, but I see no sign of moose tracks or browsing. This outer coast land is still new from glaciers. I follow the river back to the beach. The land is very clean, not even the accumulation of plastic net and rope and floats we found at Beauty Bay. Karen found one dead bird and threw it into the brush above the tide lines. Two sea otters feed and groom just offshore and a flock of black brant mutter among themselves as the sun sets and darkness settles in. Randy comes to pick us up off the shallow delta. The *Spirit* is starting to feel like a warm and secure home. We motor down the coves and coast of the east side of North Arm. A shallow cove is full of eel grass, and I can see shells below us in the clear water. But no other beaches beckon for walking, and it is rapidly getting dark. We anchor up in Quartz Bay in the last light, and Randy and I squeeze together in the tiny kitchen to make supper. It has been a long day, after a rough night. By 10:00 the generator is shut off, and we go to bed in the silence of a calm anchorage.

April 29

All is dark in the bilge, but Randy's peeping alarm rouses me. I am first up; the boat and seas quiet in the soft grey light before dawn. The battery bank provides power for the coffee pot and water for hot chocolate. As the coffee finishes brewing, I hear Don moving about in the pilot house where he bunks. I take a cup of coffee topside to him, and he invites me in. Steam rises from our cups as we sit in silence and watch the light gather around the small bay. First the snowy mountain ridges high above us, then the rocky walls with waterfalls still flowing down, then the dark spruce forest right down to the water edge; dark colors built on dark until the light is enough to reflect the *Spirit's* hull in the glassy water of the bay. This is a beautiful bay that I have wanted to explore on previous trips, but this is the first time I have been inside it. There are several small rocky islands at the entrance, somewhat protecting the waters from the swells of the Gulf. A long narrow beach rings the head of the bay, trimmed with a few spruce snags and a couple small creeks.

Thumps and sleepy voices below signal that the rest of the crew is coming awake. The beach calls strongly to me for a morning exploration. I ask Randy to run me ashore while the crew gets breakfast, before we make the run to McCarty Fjord which will be our day's work. I don't know how to run an outboard or maneuver an inflatable in ocean waters, and this lack is getting very inconvenient. We land at the west end of the beach and secure the Zodiac to a nail-studded timber we find embedded in the pebbles and sand.

Within the first few steps, I see patches of rain-beaded brown oil laid on the dark rocks. Glancing ahead, the tar balls follow the curve of the beach, scattered and thick with shells and kelp and drift twigs. As I follow the line around to the mouth of the small stream in the middle of the bay, the tar ball patches get larger, spreading out in the smaller particles of sand. The oil has only been here a day or two; its own weight flattens the balls into pancakes and presses the tar into the surface layers of sand and cobbles. Fresh otter tracks run perpendicular to the lines of tar balls, out of the woods to the sea and back again. Randy helps me collect a sample and take notes and photos. This time I manage to keep most of the oil off of me. Quietly we return to the Zodiac and motor out to the *Spirit* as the sun breaks over the mountain ridge on the east side of the bay. Soon Don pulls the anchor, and we are underway for McCarty Fjord. The day is high overcast and calm. I have the cabin to myself as I store the sample jars and record my findings on the maps.

I take my breakfast of tea and muffin on deck as we head southeast toward Harrington Point. My mind reels with the shock of finding oil so unexpectedly in Quartz Bay. It is oriented more to the south/southwest than Beauty Bay and does not receive the direct waves and wind from the southeast storm tracks. I never walked it clean, and that feels like a loss to me. This pristine, wave lashed coast, far and wild, is painfully close to the impacts of human lives.

I like quiet peaceful mornings, and the desecration on the beach hits hard. Although it is still early, I feel like I have done a day's work and want to go to some place silent and alone to find a new equilibrium. But there is no such luxury for me; questions pour over me for planning the day's work and logistics. I have to juggle and resolve the tides, weather, speed of the *Spirit* and anchoring places; match the work to be done with our different skills; select beaches to be surveyed; check the disposition of the Avon and Zodiac, making sure there is sufficient fuel and the right outboard engine; and on and on and on.

There are a couple boats waiting on the marine radio phone off Harrington Point. All have dark waterlines on their hulls. The sea lions are missing from the rocks off the point.

An eagle circles and lands high on a crag above our deck. With binoculars, I see dark brown smears on white tail feathers. Later another eagle has oil on its head. It is midmorning by the time we arrive off the long beach at James Lagoon. At least we haven't seen any oil on the water after we started up McCarty Fjord.

A long sandy beach pinches the outlet of James Lagoon against a rock wall. The tidal changes pour in and out through the narrow channel like a large river, powerful and full of standing waves. The sea otters alternate feeding in the shallows just inside and outside the lagoon entrance, often two dozen of them diving or munching clams while drifting in the eddies. The sight of heavy boom across the entrance is linear and jarring in this flowing spring place. Large black boom has been strung from rock to beach in an attempt to keep oil from flowing into the lagoon with the tide.

Sandy and Jeff pile a great heap of equipment into the Zodiac for the fisheries and water quality work. Karen and Chuck will walk both sides of the long outer beach looking for dead or sick birds and animals. I will walk the beaches at the head of the lagoon, checking our vegetation plots, collecting soil samples and mapping oil strikes. I drop onto the top of the pile in the Zodiac for a lift into the lagoon. As we will be gone for several hours, I tell Don to take the *Spirit* and go find us some fish for supper.

Sandy maneuvers the Zodiac cautiously in the swift current approaching the entrance. The boom blocks our passage into the lagoon, so we have to beach and carry the whole load and boat around. The boom is a series of large black sausages about eight or ten inches in diameter, threaded through with heavy chain and fringed with a rubber curtain that hangs into the water. On the far side I can see chain wrapped around spruce roots exposed over bedrock. The tide has just begun to ebb, and the middle of the boom is underwater from the force of the flow. I follow the chain line up through the beach ryegrass over the slight beach ridge. The force of the water has pulled the anchoring chain crosswise through the grasses, mowing them down and tearing up roots and sand.

Sandy and Jeff have reloaded the Zodiac when I return. In thigh deep water, I play tug of war with the current for the boat while Sandy and Jeff climb in and get the engine started. My foot slips on the rocks as I lurch in, and I belly flop onto the top of the gear pile, feet high over the bow, head in the bilge. We are all laughing as Sandy puts the engine in gear and pushes out into the current. Then I feel the cold wet fingers of water running off my hip boots and soaking my pants. By the time I scramble upright, the water reverses and runs down my legs inside my boots, soaking me to the waist. We are all wearing the Mustang suits, and despite the cold wind, I am warm enough for the moment. We motor around the shoal at the outflow of the lagoon and out across the waters of the hidden bay.

The weather has cleared up and only thin clouds scatter across the light blue sky. The sun is high, but the air is still cold. Spring on the coast is an illusion of light, but not temperature. Snow still rings the lagoon and rises high above us to rocky crags. Flocks of returning ducks wing low above the calm water. Sea otters peer at us over furry bellies and mussel brunches, rolling over to clean the table every few seconds. Sandy drops me off on the north end of the beach to walk the oil patrol. The head of the lagoon is a web of sea marsh and interconnecting stream channels. Quiet falls as Sandy and Jeff motor back out into the middle of the lagoon and begin their sampling protocol for water quality. The serenity of the spring morning is soothing to me, standing on the dark beach, bright orange and hip booted. I can take the time to explore thoroughly, examining each drainage and lagoon pool. Boom is festooned across the drainage channels, some white, some bright yellow. The first stream I encounter runs clear and noisy, with a waterfall somewhere up the cliff tumbling down to join it. Up around the corner, a line of white boom has been torn loose by the tide at one end and is strung uselessly along one bank. Further on the channels are deep. There are seven channels with boom; four of these are unprotected where the boom has been torn out by the tide and hangs in the current.

I carefully make my way across the maze of channels and sedges, photographing the streams and boom, locating and tagging the vegetation plots, collecting soil samples and notes. The smells of spring are rich in the air, old sedges brown and bowed by winter tides and snow, musty, dusty and pungent in the weak sunwarm. The quietness is tranquil, broken by spring birds and running or lapping water and the crunch of my boots in the gravel. The main stream in the middle is running deep and swift, but I find a shallows for crossing.

There is no evidence of oil anywhere on the beach, only land otter tracks romping from shore to water and back again. After the Quartz Bay beach, I am relieved that this beach is clean. Reaching the far end, I call for a pick up. Karen and Chuck have finished their patrol of the outer beaches and come in the small Avon to retrieve me. They report clean sands and a couple long-dead birds which were tossed into the beach grasses.

The tide is pouring out full force when we reach the entrance to the lagoon. The huge black boom is twisted and straining under water in the middle and suspended high above the surface on the south end. The whirlpools still eddy around the rock banks. Chuck skillfully guides the Avon under the boomline next to the rocks. The boom is eight or ten feet above us, twisted and futile above the current and completely non-functional for keeping oil out of the lagoon. The current rushes us out into McCarty Fjord and eddies us next to the rocks below the entrance. More of the black boom is washed up at the high tideline, black on black rocks, with "U.S. Coast Guard" stenciled white. This boom has been torn from its moorings and discarded by tides and humans.

An aluminum skiff roars past us while we examine the beached boom, three orange suited figures ignoring us and focused on the boom at the lagoon entrance. We flag them down, the first oil spill workers we have contacted directly. They are working for a VECO subcontractor, monitoring and maintaining the boom for James Lagoon. They report that EXXON doesn't seem concerned about the state of the boom, flying out every day or so and telling them to "keep at it." They have had to reset this boom four times and are frustrated because the system isn't working, and little is happening to find methods which will work. The only thing keeping James Lagoon oil-free is the lack of oil in the vicinity.

Karen, Chuck and I take the small Avon and go down the west shore of McCarty Fjord to check the pocket beaches. I hope to find how far the oil has moved up the fjord. The seas are fairly calm with a light swell running from the Gulf. Even so there is enough surf on each of the short steep beaches to get us wet as we land. After a couple clumsy efforts, we get a technique that works. Chuck brings the Avon perpendicular to the beach with Karen and I perched on the bow. At the crest of the wave, we both jump and run, while Chuck reverses the engine and backs into deeper water. Leaving the beach is tricker, because the Avon poises on the wave crests until a big swell comes in, then Chuck lets it wash in, we jump on the bow, and at the same time, push the Avon against the force of the breaker back into deeper water. This is usually a mighty running push, followed by a belly flop, landing face down somewhere between the covered bow and the anchor in the bilge. Sometimes the prop gets tangled in the kelp and quits at a critical moment. Then the whole works washes ashore broadside, water and pebbles over the stern.

We check about half the beaches between James Lagoon and Harrington Point, finding no evidence of oil. These beaches and cliffs are a wonderful collection of microcosms. Some have caves cut by wave action into the weaker bedrock. Shells and kelp and driftwood are piled high against the cliffs and into the spruce woods in hidden corners. There are sheltered clefts in the rocks, splashed with white, marking cormorant nest sites. Many species of birds wheel around us: cormorants, surf scoters, gulls, an eagle. We see three sea lions in the near shore swells and about 15 sea otters in the kelp beds. One of these is massively pregnant, huge furry belly rising from the water. Sea otters pound clams and crabs on a rock resting on their chests to break the shells to reveal dinner. I wonder how this one can keep her rock flat to break open the food she finds. We examine the prominent black lines that ring many cliffs from high tide down for several feet. They are densely packed tiny mussels, shiny black shells. I suspect that some of these areas have been reported as oil on the cliffs. But this shore, at least for now, is clean and alive, and my hope for the coast rises with every beach we check.

The swells get bigger as we reach Harrington Point. Off to the south, the *Spirit* rests above the shallow halibut spot, outlined white in the harsh sunlight on steel grey water. We head out for it, feeling very small in the larger waters, but soon we come alongside the *Spirit* and clamber up on deck. Don and Randy are skunked for halibut but have several rock bass for their efforts. We haul the Avon on board and head back to pick up the water crew who are still in the lagoon. We arrive as they come out of the entrance. The tide is at full low now, and the boom is almost entirely out of water. Jeff and Sandy have lots of room to bring the fully loaded Zodiac under the boom. Towing the Zodiac, we head up the fjord. I want to check the beach at the ranger station and then survey the head of the fjord for harbor seals. Lunch is grabbed and eaten on deck without getting out of our Mustang suits.

Don brings the *Spirit* into the little bight inside the beach moraine at the site of the ranger station. The park stations backcountry rangers here in the summer. I note the winter changes as we go ashore in the Zodiac. The beach is piled higher and steeper and the drainage channel from the pond has cut away the trail that skirted the edge of the beach. A small dark figure bursts from the ryegrass and scoots around the sandy beach, oblivious to the orange two-leggeds. The river otter rolls in the sand and runs humpbacked along the beach, then back into the ryegrass. I follow the clean beach around the curve. Little icebergs float offshore and the sun is warm on my face. Walking back to the Zodiac, the stillness is broken by a crescendoing roar on the mountain. An avalanche pours down the mountainside, leaping out over the narrow confines of the gully, then spreading in tendrils over the runout zone. White patterns on white, with scattered rocks for emphasis. The roar fades into the stillness and we leave this place for the *Spirit*.

The Zodiac tugs against the long tow rope in the wake as the *Spirit* motors up the fjord. During earlier boat and aerial surveys, we have found only a few harbor seals along the coast. During summer, there are usually concentrations of seals near the glacier faces, lounging on the icebergs or feeding below the broken brash ice. Population numbers of harbor seal have been dropping off over the past several years, but we don't really know why. I hope they haven't moved over to Prince William Sound for the spring this year. So I use this trip to check a couple fjords closely for seals.

Spirit rounds the moraine beach and we get our first view of the face of McCarty Glacier eight miles away. The blue waters of the fjord make a wide straight path between towering mountains, ending in a 200-foot wall of ice. Closer, Dinglestadt Glacier pours off the Harding Ice Field through a steep walled valley but doesn't reach the fjord waters. Other patch glaciers cling to tiny cirques high above us, fading but persistent remnants of the huge ice tongue that filled this entire valley less than two hundred years ago. The ice has retreated rapidly from its morainal rest near James Lagoon, 16 miles since 1910, and has left the steep bare walls of bedrock and deep waters. The top of the ice line shows as a faint ridge of till left by the glacier high on the mountain, rounded shoulders below, sharp crenelated aretes above. This land is still very new from the ice, still finding a comfortable shape, an equilibrium of processes. Meltwater slides down the dark grey bedrock, shining in the weak sun, sometimes bringing mudflows of gravel and clay to build toehold deltas at the water's edge. As we proceed up the fjord, the vegetation succession unfolds on the barren slopes. Outside the terminal moraine by James Lagoon mature forests of spruce and hemlock cover the mountain sides, slashed by steep avalanche paths and leaping waterfalls. Patches of tall old spruce grow on the moraine, providing perches for the eagles watching the salmon migrations. Even these outrider bastions of forest have died in places, inundated by salt water after the earthquake. At the ranger station, another small moraine provides suitable substrate for forests, but there are only widely scattered spruce among the dense alder thickets. Up-fjord, even the ubiquitous alder gives way, hanging on in scattered patches. Finally only dried grasses, sedges and forbs are scattered about, clinging to the gravel deltas at the water's edge and to till patches high in the sun below the permanent ice. Carved and burnished bedrock stretches from ice to ice, fjord surface to glacier, laced with waterfalls and speckled with goats. We sight 27 mountain goats on the slopes, moving slowly in the sun to feed on old grasses, heavy white shoulders moving surely across the cliffs. The nannies must be heavily pregnant now, as I don't see any nimble kids romping between their elders.

At last *Spirit* is surrounded by icebergs, and Don doesn't want to take the new paint job on the hull into their sharp edges. Holding three-quarters of a mile away from McCarty's towering ice face, we net ice for the fish, Sandy collects plankton, and we all examine the ice for harbor seals. But the only dark patches we see turn out to be gravel; not a single seal pokes its curious head out to watch us.

The peace and pristineness filter over my heart, carrying memories of the last time I was in this place. Then too, the sun shone brightly, dancing glints off icebergs and wavelets. Bud and I kayaked up here from the ranger station last summer. We rode the swells of the incoming tide, feeling like minute white fiberglass chips among blue and white ice giants. Occasionally, an ice mass would shift or turn over as we surfed the swells nearby, throwing a cloud of seagulls screaming into the air, only to settle back in a few minutes. The waves made a constant slurping slapping sound hitting the icebergs as we passed by, meltwater dripping off the ice. As we approached the glacier face at the head of the fjord, the low rumblings of calving ice grew louder. From our kayak perches, the face of the glacier towered over us. The ice face was awesome, soaring 150 to 200 feet above us. The dense ice was a palate of whites and blues, grading from blinding white to palest delicate blue to deep clear cobalt. We maintained a respectful distance, since the shining blue and white ice masses are unstable, tumbling a hundred feet to fall before us, sending cresting waves surging toward our kayaks.

We had spent the night in front of the glacier, on the only semi-flat ground within miles. All evening, we absorbed the process of the moving ice, a constant cascade of ice splinters and chunks thundering down. A wolverine had come to visit, sniffing among our pots laid out on the kitchen rock, peering into our tent for long moments before making her way back into the alder thickets and up the creek.

The flocks of massive icebergs and brash ice were results of an active glacier, constantly moving forward, teetering at the edge, ice columns losing balance and crashing into the water. Huge fountains of spray spurted out from the foot of the ice face, followed by concentric swells which stumbled on the shore and spent their energy on the rocks. Now the glacier is quieter as we pause on the *Spirit*, and I see the ice has moved forward and nearly covers our camp spot.

The sun has arced around to the southwest mountains, and we cannot linger any longer in this clean and sparkling iceland, almost forgetting the purpose of the trip and the grim tasks we have come to do. As soon as Sandy and Jeff finish the plankton hauls, Don powers up the *Spirit* and we turn our stern to the glacier and head back to the reality of the spreading oil cover.

East across the fjord from the ranger camp, there is a valley very recently free from glacial ice with two lakes upstream. Sandy wants to check for fish in the stream as it provides new habitat for salmon, but none have been reported there yet. We hold offshore while Sandy, Jeff and Chuck take the Zodiac ashore. Sandy has worked with new streams in Glacier Bay and can barely suppress his excitement at exploring this valley. Karen and I go ashore to walk the rocky beach for the oil and dead duck survey, but the area is still clean and peaceful. When we return to the *Spirit*, the fish patrol has disappeared and shortly the sun dips below the ridge. Immediately, a chill descends, stealing even the fantasy of warmth. Karen and I go below and work on notes and maps and start supper. It is dusk when we see the orange figures on shore again, over an hour after they estimated their return. Sandy had started up the stream and just couldn't turn back until he had seen the first lake. When they return to the *Spirit* we tease him about staying on schedule, but it is good to feel his excitement at new scientific discoveries, the expansion of life into new habitats in the midst of the death from the spreading oil. Don makes the short run down to the bight just south of Delight Beach and anchors up for the night.

Gentle grey night settles down as we cook and eat supper. Sandy's inquiry about the name of his valley prompts a great discussion. "Two new lakes valley" is neither melodious nor convenient, especially for a valley third in line after Delight and Desire. We finally settle on "Delectable." After supper, Sandy, Jeff and Chuck fill the cabin working up samples and notes. It is nearly dark when I take my cup of tea up on the bow. The silence is broken by the low murmur of voices and laughter in the cabin and streamers of waterfalls off the cliffs rising around us. Finishing my tea, I climb into the Avon, which is tied alongside without the engine, taking oars and an ammo box for a seat. Randy comes out and I tell him I'm off for a short explore around the cove. He's obviously a parent, for he steps inside the cabin and returns with a life jacket, which I had forgotten. Chuckling, I tie it on and quietly pull away from the *Spirit*.

The sky is still light above the rock walls ringing the bight. The matching mountain ridge three miles across the fjord is a dark silhouette between the gleam of water and the sky glow. The solitude and quiet feel good. Something tight within me begins to loosen, a band that seized my heart this morning in Quartz Bay. Even on a large vessel in the expanse of water wilderness we had today, my role as crew leader and scientist has bound me tight. Now the boundaries melt and I feel my soul expand to the edges of water and mountain and sky and beyond. The rhythms of the land and sea pulse around me, reflected in the gentle rocking of the Avon, the pull and swing of rowing, the drip of water off the oars. The oldness of the land and the newness of its icefree shape soothe me, the clean beaches I have walked today reassure me. My head knows that it will not last, this shining pristine labyrinth of fjords and islands and headlands webbed with water. I have seen the first brush of oil, swirling off the major river flowing along the shores. It will move again and again, lifting off in waves, spreading to new areas, leaving behind filthy footprints. Like Misty after a spring walk, bringing four muddy paws into the kitchen, leaving mud puppy marks wherever she lays down. But gently rocked in the last light reflection, I feel the power of the earth to close over the wounds, to bring tremendous energy to bear on her waters and shores. Her innate healing will surpass any puny efforts we make on her behalf. It will take time and there will be scars, but eventually the land will heal and find a new equilibrium. But even knowing this to be true, I feel a deep sorrow for the changes which are being accelerated before me.

All is quiet as I bring the Avon alongside the *Spirit*. I hand the oars and ammo box up to Randy, and he holds the ladder for me to board. We don't speak, although we are last up for the night, as we move through our respective chores getting ready for bed. Snuggled down into my sleeping bag cocoon in our bilge cave, I soon drift off to sleep.

April 30

Again I am first up in the morning. The sky glow has moved to the east, but the water is calm and no clouds show in our patch of blue above the anchorage. Hearing Don move around above me, I take coffee up to the pilot house. This silent sharing of the morning is becoming a ritual, watching the sky lighten and the reflections assemble around the boat, listening to scattered radio chatter. The crew rouses quietly and slowly, easing into a day we all know will be long and hard. I had planned to spend this day in McCarty Fjord again, working the Delight and Desire drainages on the east side. But Don reports the weather forecast for clear and calm with very light seas. I decide to survey the rocky exposed outer coast while the weather is good and leave protected waters for later. We assemble gear and clean up as Don and Randy hoist the anchor and cruise down toward McArthur Pass. Passing Moonlight Bay, there is a raft of a dozen boats against the far shore, but no one is moving out in the fjord yet.

Swinging into McArthur Pass, we sight four whales, probably humpbacks, diving and surfacing close to shore. Alternate bursts of steam rise white against the dark green forest, then a roll of grey back, then another steam burst and another. Finally the grey backs are followed by tails rising above the surface, water streaming from horizontal flukes, and they sound from our sight. The rugged steep mountains above the water's surface continue on below, another whole world we can't see. But I wonder about rising mountain slopes, hidden valleys, morainal ridges and scattered boulders inhabited by whales and halibut and shrimp and plankton, visited by seals and sea otters.

In McArthur Cove, we raise the *Jessi Girl*, our bird rescue boat which has come to collect any dead birds and animals we find. I had planned for them to follow several hours behind us, cleaning up the beaches after our surveys. But thankfully, we have not found a single oiled bird carcass. The skipper of the *Jessi Girl* gives us the update on the cleanup work. There are separate fleets of bird and otter rescue boats. These crews patrol the coastal waters in skiffs or small fishing boats, looking for sick birds, which are captured and transported to the bird rescue center in Seward. Dead birds are collected from the water, but that seems to be secondary work. Establishment of the Seward otter rescue center is still in controversy, so sick otters are taken to Valdez. Oil has heavily impacted the Pye Islands, just south of McArthur Pass, and is plastering Gore Point. The thick slimy tar pools up in the protected rocky coves and hooks of the islands. Actual shore cleanup has not really begun; efforts are still focused on skimming oil off the water and trying to boom off critical salmon spawning streams.

Leaving the *Jessi Girl*, we go through McArthur Pass narrows. Streamers of sheen and mousse cover the water, gleaming dully in the morning sun. Kelp, logs, feathers, hemlock needles and plastic debris are tangled with the mousse, stained dark reddish brown in the tide rips. As we pass east through the narrows, the swells are running one to two feet, the blue sky streaky with white clouds and the sun bright enough to make me squint. The first rocky coves east of McArthur Pass are small, studded with rocks, and spaced by vertical headlands. A bird rescue boat, the *Silver Drift*, is already working Chance Cove, bobbing in the swells near the rocks. Don doesn't want to maneuver the *Spirit* in close quarters with another vessel, so we pass on to the next tiny cove.

Bobbing up and down, we lower the Zodiac and engine, and Karen, Mike, Chuck and I bumble down the ladder in full Mustang regalia. We move over close to the rocks and start patrolling around the shore. High in the spray line on the granite boulders we see shiny dark brown patches. We still don't know the appearance of oil on various substrates, and these patches look as though tar balls and mousse gobs have been thrown high by the spray and pounded by the breaking waves. But the swells give us an elevator ride up and down the wet rock faces and access looks poor.

Finally we round the corner and find a sloping ledge leading up from the high swell level. Chuck volunteers to jump out and check the dark patches on the sea side of the rocks. Mike brings the Zodiac carefully alongside as the waves push us into the boulders, then pull us away in the foam. Chuck is perched on the bow, waiting for a good chance to leap out onto the narrow ledge. Finally the Zodiac pauses imperceptibly at the top of a wave, and Chuck springs out. His landing is good and he sprints up the rocks above the spray. We follow him back around and watch him carefully make his way down to the dark brown stain against the rocks. His hip boots seek out any foothold on the steep side, hands reach out to touch reassuring rock, then he bends over to touch the stain. I expect to see his fingers turned to us, brown from the blot. But he rubs his hands against the patch, then flashes clean hands at us. Over the roar of breaking waves he yells "Its algae!" I sigh in relief. Chuck turns back up the rocks, and we meet him at the ledge on the back side. Reversing the landing process is even trickier, but Chuck makes another successful leap, and Karen and I grab his suit as he comes aboard.

Mike takes us on into the back of the cove past more huge boulders broken from the bedrock walls, wave washed, and occasionally spotted with similar brown stains. The *Silver Drift* enters the cove too, crowding *Spirit* and earning Don's ire. There is a small steep beach of round granite boulders in the northeast corner of the cove. On the earlier voyage taken by Anne and Bud, they reported rocks that were clean on top with the oil only visible by turning them over. I know Anne is going to ask me if we turned over rocks to check for oil; cruising along shore in the inflatable is not enough. Although the surf is breaking waist high on me, Mike guides the Zodiac close to the beach. Balanced on the bow, I leap and run at the critical instant, backwashing surf tugging at my ankles. The rocks range from watermelon to orange size, glistening white and black and being rolled forward and back by every breaking wave. The area is less than 50 feet long, and I walk the length, dutifully turning over boulders. But no oil is visible, even when I dig down through several layers of rocks. Then the challenge of reembarking the Zodiac. Mike kicks the engine into reverse and pulls me out of the hissing surf and tumbling green water with exquisite timing.

We decide to take the Zodiac east to Black Bay without going back aboard the *Spirit*. We explore the rest of the shore filled with tiny coves, rock walls and thundering surf. In one of the coves, we come quite close to a sea otter pulled out on a rock and spend some time watching her for signs of oil or illness. But she slips into the water, watching us without apparent fear, and we assume that she is fine. Then out into the Gulf waters around the exposed headland. The *Spirit* parallels us in deeper water as we examine the rocky islets. In past days, this area was a popular sea lion haulout, but the population has been declining, and most of the rocks are inhabited only by kelp and gulls and the myriad of marine lifeforms that somehow thrive in storm pounded niches. Out here the swells seem large. Sometimes only the pilot house and antennas show of the *Spirit*, although she has two stories above the deck. Here, at the northern edge of the Pacific Ocean, I glimpse the immense energy and expanse of water which reaches clear down the planet; from our tiny wave tossed Zodiac over eight thousand miles to Antarctica.

Off the end of Steep Point more offshore rocks thrust above the surface. A huge sea lion beach master has humped his enormous bulk up the sloping rock and peers down at us from his domain above the spray. His fur has dried golden brown from the sun, black flippers merging with the rock. His mass, probably reaching 2000 pounds, seems to be without bones, held in minimal shape by the confines of his skin. He is solitary ashore, and we see three sleek heads of cows swimming below his perch. It takes us a long time to circumnavigate the rocky headland, as we are using a 15-horse engine for the Zodiac. At least it runs, for this is no place to be adrift without power. Tired of watching our slow progress, the bull lurches down to the water's edge and is transformed into a sleek and graceful being. Mike and I glance at each other, remembering the sea lion swimming toward *Tin Lizzy* in the entrance to Pederson Lagoon on the last trip. But we round the cape and enter Black Bay without seeing him again.

We sight three sea otters on the rocks between the cape and the first beach. Sea otters have very dense fur which keeps them warm by trapping a layer of air next to their skins. Most marine mammals keep warm by a layer of insulating blubber, but for the sea otter, clean fur which keeps its loft is a matter of life and death. Many sea otters are dying from hypothermia when the oil soaks their fur and plasters it to their skin. Sea otters must also maintain a high rate of metabolism to stay warm and active, so they eat large quantities of fish, clams, sea urchins, crabs and mollusks. It is unusual for sea otters to be out of water, especially when the weather is good. Mike slows down and we watch these otters carefully. Two slip into the water, popping up their heads to watch us. But the third seems to have a patch of dark substance on its rear haunch which may be oil. And it is very slow to go into the water.

I ask Mike to put us onto the first beach inside Black Bay. It is steep and rocky, composed of granite boulders, reaching from waterline up to a thick dense tangle of drift logs and storm debris. The map shows a lake in the valley behind the beach. As we approach, the sun shines on white granite, ringed by dark green spruce forest, hedged at the ends by steep cliffs and backed by mountains and blue sky. It is truly a glorious spot and I look forward to stretching my legs and exploring. This beach has the same orientation as the Beauty Bay beach where we found oil two days ago, but that is many miles away. The surf rolls in, low and calm for this location, still waist deep on me. Mike brings us close where the surf seems smallest. This time Karen, Chuck and I are all teetering on the bow for landing. Those with knee boots go first, followed by hip boots. Green water and white foam curl around my feet as I land and turn to give the Zodiac a mighty push back into deeper water. Yet another drawback of the complex sampling gear is evident here. We need both hands free to come and go from the shore and cannot be burdened with parcels, camera cases, folders or even packs.

We start up the gleaming beach in a setting from the cover of a travel brochure. The rocks are white with sparkling black mica flecks, rolled round by countless storms. I pause to examine a rock where the dark spots seem larger than normal. My finger comes away with a dark black-brown stain where I touch the rock. Looking closer, I see dripping spots scattered all around me. On my knees, I reach for a boulder and turn it over. Thick black grease coats the entire underside. The rocks below the surface are covered, and it is pooled like blackstrap molasses in the interstices. Numbly, I release the rock and look for Karen and Chuck. They are above me on the beach, just finding spattered rocks for themselves. Chuck holds up a dark rag for me to see and shouts that it is a bird. The brightness of the day suddenly feels glaring, and the walking turns from the delight of exploring a new beach to the task of documenting destruction. We meet together by a large boulder. I will collect oil samples, Karen keeps clean to run cameras. Chuck will walk the beach and survey for dead birds and animals. I radio Don that we have found oil and will be here for awhile. Sandy and Jeff prepare for water and fisheries sampling off the beach.

Alone, I walk the north section of beach, trying to determine how high and long and deep the oil is spread. I find mousse splattered rocks all the way to the ending cliffs, and a wide band of rocks about normal high tide line reveal heavy oil when overturned. I select a spot near the large boulder to collect a sample of oil and drop to my knees in the rocks. My hands are clean as I pull out the sample jar set and unwrap the trowel. Carefully setting aside the upper layer of rocks, I try to scrape off oil for the jars. It is very thick, the consistency of bearing grease or warm fudge or cold honey. Below the surface rock, it covers the lower layers completely, enrobing them like expensive hand-dipped chocolate candies. These rocks are one to two feet thick; then an impenetrable layer of sand catches the pooling oil and it is running down-beach to the ocean. The trowel is practically worthless, too big to get between rocks, scraping off only a thin film of oil. The oil spreads onto the handle, all around the rim of the jar, onto my fingers. Finally I abandon the trowel and use rock slivers to work out enough of the mousse for a sample. I move aside more rocks, working my way down to the sand layer. My hands become slippery from the oil, and I have to grip the jars and rocks tightly to keep from dropping them.

I pause between filling the sample jars and glance down in the hole where I am working. My hands are splotched with black brown goo nearly to the wrist. The sunlight glances off the mica in the rocks and the gold of my new wedding ring.

Horrified, I look at myself, the ooze on my hands and boots, tar smeared on my knees. My heart contracts at the sight of the ring. Barely six weeks ago our friend, Steve Ortland, spent days making it; creating out of Bud's idea and two golds, this symbol of our commitment to each other. The rings rested heavy and glimmering in Steve's hand as he brought them to us while we dressed for the wedding, bare hours before the ceremony. As we descended the stairs to join our family and friends, the soft white silk of my wedding dress swirled around my feet, and the beads and sequins sparkled in the light of the candles Bud and I carried. After joyful poems and heartfelt vows, Steve handed the rings to Ketki, our "minister of choice," who blessed them in the candle-lit room and handed them to Bud and I. Bud took the tiny circle of mountains and clouds and tried to push it onto my finger upside down. Now I am shaken at the sight of it smeared with black tar, today's reality clashing with the fairy tale wedding. Again the ring becomes a symbol: shining hopes for our future and this pristine coast, now tarnished dully with human waste.

The veneer of scientist is tattered as I complete the collection. The flimsy green card and marker are out of the question, so I smear the sample item number on a granite rock with oil. Karen photographs me working there in the black hole, an intent figure in orange suit. I clean my hands by wiping them down the rough rocks, then using absorbent pads. My hands are still stained brown and feel greasy, but it is the best I can do. I want to get away from the oil, escape to my clean and springlit land. But the oil on my boots and the scratches in my ring will go with me.

Karen tells me there are quite a few dead birds on the beach. Most have been scavenged by predators. The *Silver Drift* comes along shore. I radio Don to ask if they will collect the dead birds here after we have inventoried and identified them. The men are amenable and even bring extra absorbent pads ashore for me to clean up. Chuck and Karen found a dead bald eagle in the tidal debris line and collect it. It is found with clutched talons and outspread neck. Otherwise, we do not find a complete bird anywhere on the beach. Wings and heads are jammed between the boulders, oily black remnants from scavengers. All are sodden black with bloody bare breast bones. Feathers are stuck to the rocks and drift logs with blood and oil. Chuck and Karen only hazard guesses as to their identity.

I climb up to the storm debris line at the top of the beach while Karen and Chuck are finishing up. The drift logs are huge, layered with gravel and plastic. This beach catches full force of storms and is built and torn down by lashing waves and the flotsam they bring. Carefully, I climb among the jackstraw tangle. As promised by the map, a small lake surrounded by bedrock and forest is nestled in the valley. The lake is still ice locked and would be too small to land on anyway. This is a difficult location to reach and despite the work bringing me there, I find it beautiful as I rest at the end of an upthrust log in the maze. A river otter at the ocean's edge catches my eye, and I watch it run with arching back up through the granite rocks and into the woodpile. I find a large pink plastic float. Don had requested a couple if we found them, so I bring it down. It bounces high after I heave it over the debris pile, ricochetting crazily between the boulders and rolling to a stop near the waves.

Karen and Chuck are assembling the gear down by the shore, and Mike detaches the Zodiac from *Spirit* and comes in. Three times he brings the bow of the Zodiac in, and scientist and samples scramble aboard. I have my hands full wrestling with the float, but we all make it off the beach safe and dry. We decide to continue around the shore of Black Bay in the Zodiac to check other beaches.

It is becoming very obvious to me that oil cannot be reliably mapped from aerial or water platforms. We need to walk beaches to accurately locate oil contamination. It comes in many guises, depending on weathering, substrate and time in the water. There is no primer on oil states in northern marine environments. We are learning it as we go, teaching ourselves the colors, the smell, the consistency, the distribution, the effects. Each beach, oiled or not, adds to our knowledge of the patterns.

There are two or three small pocket beaches as we go north. However the surf is getting bumptious, and we pass them by. We go around a corner and find a hidden strand of boulders in the quiet backwater. This should be clean, according to my ever changing theories of oil strike prediction. It's in the back of a bay, faces away from the main currents, is quiet . . . But it is accessible so we all go ashore, and scramble over the slippery boulders. Oil splatters! So much for that theory.

Before leaving Seward, Karen Gustin, the chief interpreter for the park, asked me to bring her examples of oiled and unoiled items from the coast for a display. There are smallish granite rocks here, so I range through the debris piles looking for a bucket to carry some back. The drift logs have been pushed right into the vegetation, hemlock and salmon berry bushes growing over the old wood. I clamber up on a huge log and peer into a swirl deposit of detergent bottles, fishing floats, twigs, kelp, shells and grasses. "This is a good place for a glass ball," I think, as I teeter on the log six feet above the flotsam nest. Then climbing down, there it is at my feet! Partially covered with sea debris, a round and whole green glass Japanese fishing float. Glee bubbles in me as I stoop to pick it up. Fragile sphere traveler of long ocean miles, past rocky coasts, over boulder beach, laid by some huge high wave onto this bed of kelp and grasses. It feels smooth and cool in my hands which are scratched raw from rocks and grimy with oil. I see the rope net pattern where water and sand have etched the glass. Round. Whole. Fragile. It feels like a gift from the sea. I tuck it inside my shirt and turn to work again. But these few moments remind me that this immense and sometimes violent land can also be gentle and nurturing.

It is early afternoon by the time we are all assembled on the *Spirit* again. Looking at the map, I have decided to check Thunder and Two Arm Bays further east. So we leave the quiet of Black Bay and are on the outer coast again. There are several narrow exposed beaches footing the cliffs between Black and Thunder Bays. But even in the relatively calm seas of today, the surf is too high to land, though I am pretty sure they have been oiled.

There are four beaches at the head of Thunder Bay, and I decide to check two. Karen and I go ashore on the first one. It too has a small lagoon lake sheltered behind the beach ridge. The drainage runs crystal clear, colored stones on the bed of the stream. We walk parallel along the beach at different tide drift lines. She calls me over when she finds a dead bird in the last tide line. Unlike the birds at Black Bay, this one has not been scavenged and has a light smear of oil across the white breast feathers. Karen identifies it as an ancient murrelet and begins the routine of photographing and note taking which accompanies collection of specimens. While she is working on the documentation, I continue along the lower kelp line. Something gleaming bright in the tangled golden brown kelp catches my eye. Thinking I've spotted a piece of glass or wet shell, I push aside the kelp with my hand and look in shock at the brown stains on my fingers. Then I see many such shiny objects in the kelp. They are tar balls which came ashore in the debris with the last tide. The sun is hot on the beach and the tar balls are melting. They are almost pretty; dark brown black, shiny bright as Christmas ornaments, winking up from the dowdy kelp and driftwood. Following the tideline, they appear more numerous, ranging in size from walnuts to cantaloupes. When I mar their surface, the glistening reflection becomes a green-brown goo, not unlike baby shit. They are melting even as I walk the beach, oozing from their kelp beds into the sand and gravel beneath, spreading wider and deeper into the substrate. When I pick up handfuls of kelp with tar balls, stringy strands trail off to the beach, like hot black mozzarella cheese. The clean salty sea scent is gone, overridden by a spoiled, rotting smell which clings to my nostrils.

Subdued, I radio to the *Spirit* that we have located oil after all. Don tells me that he has been watching four immature bald eagles feeding on the next beach north of us. Sandy, Jeff and Chuck go ashore and report an oiled sea otter carcass at the latest tideline. By the time Karen and I finish and Mike takes us to that beach, the original crew has begun the collection process for the carcass. The eagles perch in tall spruce just back of the beach watching, occasionally screeching at us. I begin to walk the kelpline and immediately find more tar balls melting into the gravel.

Then off to the south, I hear the unmistakable whop whop whop of an approaching helicopter. Soon a Jet Ranger swings along the beach and settles in to land on the next beach north. I recognize the tail numbers of the ADEC bird. They generally fly the shoreline at low tide, trying to map oil extent offshore and where it has hit the beaches. In some places, they land the helicopter above the high tide line and run an in-depth transect. I want to talk with them, to find out what they're seeing on their surveys. It would be valuable to correlate our ground survey with their aerial work. Mike comes into shore, and I hop onto the bow of the Zodiac. As we slowly approach the shore where ADEC landed, they all climb back into their helicopter and close the doors. We're hardly invisible in the big Zodiac with bright orange suits, but the helicopter remains sealed up while I land and start up the beach. Then a man comes to meet me and I recognize Roy Warren who had been working in Prince William Sound before moving here.

He tells me they mapped this beach and all other beaches in Thunder Bay as "no oil." I tell him of the tar balls we've found, which of course are not visible from the helicopter. They are basing the ranking on Prince William Sound, using a modification of a system developed for the AMOCO oil spill in Brittany, France in 1978. Relatively speaking, perhaps there is little oil on these beaches, but there is enough to soil the kelp lines and kill otters and birds. Roy tells me of the oiling in the Pye Islands and says that Bud was out with them the day before. Oil is swirled in the rocky hooks there one to two feet thick on the water. Roy asks if I want any messages taken to town. I have no technical messages to pass along as the work is going well. I really want Bud to have been on board that helicopter, even if we would have had only brief minutes for a hug buffered by Mustang suits. "Just tell Bud that I love him." After the helicopter lifts off and its noisy engine fades in the east, I walk this beach alone. Here too, I find scattered shiny black tar balls. Three beaches for three, in the back of a sheltered bay I thought would be clean.

The crew retrieving the sea otter gets ferried back to the *Spirit* in the Avon, and Don brings the *Spirit* over to pick us up. Although the sea otter is wrapped in multiple layers of heavy plastic bags and stored in a large garbage can, the back deck is aromatic. I shudder to think of collecting dead birds for days at a time. Don is sober when Karen shows him the ancient murrelet. There are people for whom the highlight of their trip to Alaska is the sight of an ancient murrelet during one of his Kenai Fjords tours.

A plane is supposed to come out to meet us tomorrow, returning Karen and samples to Seward, and hopefully, bringing Bud to join the crew for a few days. As yet we still do not have a functioning radio system on the outer coast beyond regular marine channels. We need to know when the plane is coming and to tell them where to meet us. Don requests a message relay to Seward. Although we cannot talk with the chain of boats, we can hear most of the process. The message is repeated through four boats until it reaches a cannery office in Seward. The operator there calls the park office, gets the information, then reverses the process through all four boats to us again. Like playing Pass the Secret, only all the players can hear each version. The messages remain remarkably intact.

Although it is now late afternoon, I want to see some of Two Arm Bay while the weather is still good. The importance of calm seas is not lost on me as I hop on and off the Zodiac at each beach, and I want to cover as much ground as possible while the seas cooperate. So we head further east, past another short stretch of exposed cliff coast, then around Cloudy Cape and into Taroka Arm of Two Arm Bay.

The head of Taroka Arm is hammer-head shaped, a long blunt indentation in the coast with small coves and streams at either side. A long beach borders the mountains at the west end, curling a shielding gravel spit around a small, deep and very protected cove. A steep-sided valley stretches west from the cove, and last sunlight is streaming through a cut in the mountains at its head. The north side of the valley is made of a humongous avalanche path, wide runout zone skirting the lower slopes, rising through narrow gullies to steep cliffs that catch the clouds. Even in the gathering evening chill, we hear the distant rumble of high avalanches. They are running wet spring snow, loosened by direct sun weaving tendrils on tendrils in the runout cone. The steep lower slopes behind the beach are already patchy snowfree, dun and gold with old grasses and bare alder.

Karen, Chuck and I go ashore on the long beach. Walking up to the tideline, the rocks appear clean and the kelp line stretches away on either side. However just below the kelp, I spot small splatters on the dark rocks and find oil beneath my knees. Moving cobbles aside, oil extends down into the beach. Turning over the kelp, the melted tar balls glitter. The kelp line is completely soaked with tar and mousse, dripping from the stick I use to lift it. We spread out to check more of the beach. The full length of the strand is saturated. The west end of the beach has large jagged boulders brought down by avalanches. The kelp sponge has been laid on these rocks by the tide. Oil has melted and flowed out of the kelp, dripping down the facets, pooled in the crevices. The tentacles reach over the boulders, logs and kelp toward the ocean waters that brought the oil here. The color is varied and rich, polished by the afternoon sun. Warm browns, with a tinge of red, wound through with streaks of shiny black, contrasting with the dark dull greys of the rocks.

Carefully, I collect a sample. Karen burns up film. Sandy and Jeff go through their water sampling protocol off the decks of the *Spirit*. I want to check the other beach and cove on the opposite side of the arm and call to Karen that it is time to go. But she is deep in photography, catching the last light.

"Just a couple more," she calls, and then a couple more. I am torn because her photos are valuable, but we need to check the rest of the arm and night is coming on. Finally she comes running, awkward in her bulky orange suit, putting cameras away as she crunches down the beach.

We take the Zodiac across the bay to check the beach and cove on the opposite side of the arm. As we follow the shore around, Karen spots a black bear behind a large drift log on the narrow beach. It appears to be feeding on something, head down for long moments, then peering myopically over the log, nose searching for smells from the sea. Then back behind the log, head down, rear up, intent on spring breakfast. We watch it awhile, then they take me over to the beach.

This beach stretches over a mile along the east side of Taroka Arm. The north end has a low bedrock knob with stunted vegetation, ideal for trolls or even humans who want a campsite with a view. A small black sand beach is nearly covered with drift logs, woven with poly rope and net in gay colors. I have a theory that the oil should be deposited with the large accumulations of drift logs, since that is obviously where flotsam is deposited by the currents, and Black Bay was a great example of it. So I start by examining the beach near the heap of drift logs. The beach is clean at the north end, and the wet sand is braided with tracks of river otter and seabirds. Further, fox or coyote tracks join the parade. Then I find where a sow bear and two cubs finished their beach patrol and climbed up into the thickets above the storm tide line. My senses are sharpened as I follow their tracks backward down the beach. They have walked the tidelines, weaving between the last two or three kelp lines, looking for carrion to augment a diet of green shoots and roots. The flotsam line is sparse around the small cliff, a thin line of kelp, twigs, mussel shells and seeds. Then a shiny blob gleams in the dark sand, a tar ball spread out like a dead jellyfish. Then another and another. And the otter and gull and bear tracks follow the deadly line which should be the dinner table. Again and again, the cub tracks narrowly miss the sticky tar balls. But how long can even a mother bear keep two lively cubs from romping away? Their tracks dash up and down, and then step right in the oil. I imagine them full of curiosity and mischief, in a world of new smells and sights. After all, they've spent the first months of life cooped up in a small den, and now they're making up for lost time. My heart is in turmoil as I absorb the ecological significance of the bears searching the oil for food. I blatantly humanize the sow bear, smiling as I imagine her telling the cubs to wipe their paws clean before going back into the den.

I find more and more oil as I follow the beach south. First the melted tar balls in the sand, like dropped and forgotten ice cream. Then mousse tossed on drift logs, dripping down the sides from the sun. Then the saturated kelp mass, six inches deep, a foot or two across, a mile or more long. Here too, the tar has rolled up with the kelp at sea, then been deposited by the tide and melted into the cobbles by the hot sun. It is starting to run downbeach to the water line. But it has only been here a day or two at most, and if I had a rake and garbage sacks, I could roll it up and take it away. A huge log lies prone on the beach, root maze draped with poly net. The net is weathered and bristly with lines, faint green and hoary white. And covered with black brown oil from the waterline down to the beach. The oil covered water was a good foot and a half deep here, and it painted the net with mousse as the tide subsided. I have noticed that the polypropylene net and rope debris are often oil soaked, as though like attracts like.

I am in shock, and suddenly unutterably weary as I continue on down the beach. The oiled cobbles and dripping kelp line extend in front of me, a mile or more, until the beach terminates at the fjord cliff walls. The bear tracks continue before me, weaving between sand patch and cobbles, always along the oily kelp. I am alert to rustles in the beach ryegrass above the beach and smells brought to me by the sea breeze, in case the sow decides to check the beach again. I walk over a half mile, shambling between tide lines. The sun slips below the mountain ridge across the arm, and I have seen all I can for one day. Drained, I sit on the end of a clean log and radio for Karen and Chuck to come pick me up. Soon the hum of the engine on the Zodiac approaches, and I wade out to meet them.

They report the small beach inside the cove at the northeast head of the arm as clean. They were holding offshore near the *Spirit*, watching the bear. Karen had hoped to go ashore and see what it was feeding on, but the bear is resting on the log, and doesn't feel the need to cooperate with invading scientists. They saw two other black bear on the slopes; with the tracks of the sow and two cubs I followed, it totals six for the head of this arm. Taroka means "black bear," and this isolated arm is a spring gathering place for them. The early snowfree slopes grow green shoots and rich roots for spring grazing. The long beaches accumulate winterkill, washed up by the currents and deposited on the doorstep. Over the next several months the snowbanks at the base of the avalanches will melt back slowly, creating a zone of perpetual spring at the edge, where succulent greens sprout anew all summer long. The streams provide spawning habitat for salmon runs. In fall the alpine slopes brim with blueberries, salmonberries, huckleberries, mossberries, voles and ants. Then the rocks and trees provide warm shelter near timberline for winter dens.

Don is chuckling as I climb onto the deck of the *Spirit*. He tells me that the bear had scooped snow from the avalanche track onto the big drift log, then laid down on the log for a snooze, with its fore paws *on* the snow pile. I laugh with him, figuring it's a wild tale he has concocted to watch the scientist scurry to her notes and camera. Through binoculars, I watch the bear leisurely rise from the log, amble up through the alders and begin to graze on new grasses. And on the log there is a small pile of snow with meltwater dripping down the sides!

I decide to make the run back to McCarty Fjord, as we need to resume work at Delight and Desire valleys the next day and I don't want to get stuck if the weather comes up. There is barely time to make the run back before full dark is upon us. Don powers *Spirit* up to cruising speed and heads out the arm as we all catch up on notes, maps and samples in the cabin. I climb up to the pilot house as *Spirit* rounds the cape and heads southwest along the outer coast. Standing in the open doorway on the lee side, I brace against the swell. Ocean and mountain merge in a froth of surf from the Pacific. Overhead, the sunset paints the scattered clouds with pink and golden streaks. The light is reflected on the crests of the waves below us, frosted with white caps, edged with cliffs on one side, limitless ocean to the south.

I am exhausted as I stand in the quiet of the pilot house, background of powerful diesel engines, and low radio chatter, hiss of water along the bow. I am overwhelmed by sorrow and fatigue. Hope drains out of me like water seeping out of a cracked pottery jar. In the space of a few-12 hour tide cycles, the coast has become tainted. Tears flow down my face onto the deck and overboard to mingle with waves tossed in the sunset light. So many beaches. Beauty Bay was not just an isolated oil hit, but one of a huge puzzle. And I am exhausted mentally, physically and emotionally from disentangling that puzzle bay by bay, beach by beach; and from planning and coordinating the logistics and work of the team. Scientist and team leader recede, leaving the child of the land. The glorious pristine solitude is gone as the land changes rapidly all around me. Even the water beneath us continues to carry oil to the beaches, the perpetual tides spreading it anew. I have seen the dead animals and the scavengers feeding on their carcasses. I have watched the oily sheen, the glistening tar balls, the dripping mousse like old blood from wounds.

For so many years this land has nurtured and cared for me, held me gently, shown me beauties and strengths, led me to adventures. But now she is in great pain, assaulted by an incurable illness, and I feel like it has become my task to care for her. I need to decide which beaches can be cleaned and which ones are to be left because cleanup will be too damaging or simply not possible. Like a child who becomes an adult and comes to care for her own elderly parents, the roles of nurturing are reversed.

Spirit slips into the bight south of Delight beach again for the night. The mountains are dark around us and deep blue sky caps our anchorage. The color reminds me of an Eskimo man's description of blue during a discussion of Yupik words and their English interpretation. After several attempts to convey his meaning, he burst out "It's pitch blue. You know--like pitch black." So we have pitch blue sky and twinkling stars overhead as the engines are turned off, and we all go below to the chores of supper. Again Randy and I are chefs. Others seem somewhat intimated by the kitchen, although they are ready enough for cleanup chores.

After supper, I settle back to read a little, and my wedding photo falls out of the pages. I examine the smiling faces but feel no connection to those people. I keep trying to reach through to their eyes. Nothing. The words on the pages dance before my eyes too, and I can't grasp the gist of the travels through China that I'm reading about. I give it up and go below to my sleeping bag. My sleep this night is troubled by nightmares. Horrible images of surging black tar rising up from the beach and coming to engulf me. Vague dark mists drifting over the land and out to sea. Tar pits trapping my boots. And the helpless feeling of a small child who can't run and can't scream.

May 1

I am tired when I arise and go up to a silent cabin in the faint silver grey dawnlight. When I hear Don moving around above me, I carry hot chocolate and coffee to the pilot house. The day comes on blue and calm and glorious. Bud calls these "bluebird days." We are in cool shadow long after the mountains across the fjord are morning-lit. Today we will stay in McCarty Fjord and Sandy can sample the valuable fisheries drainages of Delight and Desire Creeks. I will examine Mc-

Carty Lagoon and the beaches. We overworked Mike yesterday, so he can take it easy today.

The Harbor Air plane to pick up Karen and deliver Bud is supposed to meet us at Delight Spit this morning. I am looking forward to a couple days with Bud on the coast again, even under these circumstances. Karen, Chuck and I prepare the specimens for transport, carefully wrapping the legacy of our work to turn over to the investigators. The dead eagle, the ancient murrelet, the redolent sea otter, bottles of water, plankton, oil and gravel samples. Today I have time to rest and reflect on what we have found. Just before we left, the Resources MAC group was turning its attention to beach cleanup. I feel some urgency at getting a list of oiling and possible cleanup areas to Anne so EXXON can get started immediately before the tide and sun spread the tar balls further. Sitting on the upper deck in the sun, I scribble out a letter to Anne to be delivered by Karen when she flies to town. I describe what we have seen and give a list of beaches for immediate cleanup. Then I think through the impacts of the oiling on the system.

The old adage "everything is connected to everything" was never so true as in the case of pervasive oil coating water, shore and ocean bottom. The effects of the oil spill go beyond the immediate first splash on shore or the surface layer of water visible from boat or airplane. The impacts extend in space and time throughout the water column, touching water, plants and animals from water surface to the ocean bottom, throughout the intertidal zone, up on shore and into the forests and mountains. Even the air is subject to evaporated hydrocarbons.

Oil in the water column sinking to the deep ocean floor moves into the zone of rock fish, halibut and crab. These foods become unfit for human consumption. Oil on the water surface coats seabird feathers. After preening, this oil is ingested. Often these birds die, and the carcasses wash ashore. Here they are food for scavenging eagles and bear. Oil compounds in the water column are taken in by mussels attached to rock in the intertidal zone. Toxins are concentrated in the tissue of mussels, which then become food for foragers such as river otter, sea otter, wolverine or coyotes. Oil scum driven into the storm tide zone onshore coats vegetation and soaks into the sandy soils of the storm tide meadows. Black bears feed on the plants in this area.

The entire region functions as a complex system with interconnecting processes and energy transfer throughout. Some effects of the oil impact will be felt immediately, such as lighter carbon compounds dissolved in the air and various hydrocarbons distributed through the water column and on the surface. Other effects take slightly longer: sea otters and sea birds become oil coated and die in days; within a couple weeks, plankton and fish become affected; in one to two months the intertidal zone begins to show effects. As migratory birds arrive and begin rafting and nesting in spring, they encounter oil on the water, shores and in their food. Marine mammals such as whales and porpoises accumulate oil compounds in their bodies. Bears, eagles, river otter, deer, which all feed in or near the intertidal zone, will show impacts in varying time frames.

Impacts on individuals are felt fairly soon. Impacts to populations and systems take longer to become evident and last longer. While individuals may be able to survive some oiled environment, effects may become evident in smaller, weaker young, lack of reproductive success, or sterility in later generations. Community composition will change as some species cannot tolerate oiled conditions and niches will open for other species.

Randy takes me ashore to walk the Delight beach. I am alone for the full length, even the oyster catchers and crows are absent. The beach is as clean as when Mike and I walked it a month earlier. But now in the wave and wind swept dunes I find the first green leaves of spring. The beach ryegrass pokes sharp dark leaves up from buried roots, each leaf still sheathed against wind and cold. Soon enough, they will grow full size, thrusting heavy seed heads two to three feet above the sand. Their roots and old leaves help stabilize the winter-mobile sand. The beach greens also raise brave tender leaves, circles of green in the dark sand. This beach has the largest barnacle shells I have seen along the coast, each one looking like a empty miniature volcano. Most of the shells are concentrated in the stretch near the outlet of McCarty Lagoon. I walk the full length of the beach out and back, then splash across the creek to check the vegetation plot Mike and I laid out on the previous trip. This time the creek has thawed enough to be free flowing. And not five feet from the plot, tall orange boom spans the drainage. It is curtain boom, apparently supposed to lie down when the water is flowing out and stand up vertical when the tide reverses and flows upstream. It is secured to a standing spruce snag on one side and an old drift log on the other. Trampling and tracks cover the area. Lengths of white sausage boom are strewn about. Some have broken open and trickles of white absorbent material scatter like snow. Just cleaning up the paraphernalia of this cleanup is going to be an effort.

Walking back to the spit, I stop to examine the boom which has been placed across the entrance to McCarty Lagoon. This boom is constructed of large spruce logs, joined together with links of heavy chain. Absorbent fringes are tacked along the lower inside edge to catch oil which may get under the boom or between the logs. The tide is running out in full ebb, and the line of boom is bellied out with the current, but it lies on the surface of the water, all the way to the beaches. The chain strains where it is wrapped around roots of drift trees, but the boom does not gap above the water. In all the streams I have seen, this is the only boom which is truly functioning.

Randy picks me up off the beach in the Avon. When I reach the *Spirit*, Harbor Air flies over, radioing Don that he has a full load and can't pick up Karen until the afternoon.

Mike is stirring and agrees to go into the lagoon with me to check for oil on the shores. We have to carry the Avon over the boom on shore, then motor through the swift shallow water in the bottleneck and into the quiet waters of the inner lagoon. McCarty Lagoon is an oblong shaped deep bowl tucked back into the mountain ridges. The sides of the cove rise steep from the water surface, streaked with avalanche tracks and jumbled boulders. Several eagles nest in tall spruce in here, feeding on the rich red salmon run in Delight Creek. As we slowly patrol the shores, Mike spots an eagle feeding on the beach. Leaving Mike in the Avon to keep it offshore in the dropping tide, I wade ashore. The eagle is intent on her dinner, tugging this way and that, hopping back and forth, tearing off morsels of flesh. I want to check the carcass to see if oiled animals have drifted into the lagoon. The eagle flies up to a nearby spruce as I slowly approach. She is feeding on a large red wolf eel with a huge block head and narrow long dorsal fin. I check it over carefully, but see no evidence of oil on the body or the nearby rocks. The eagle swoops down behind me as I go on inland up the cobble beach. I check several kelp lines and walk to the end of the beach by the stream coming out near the cliffs. Not a sign of oil anywhere. The tide continues to ebb and Mike has pushed the Avon further out as I return. We have to pole it out to deep water to avoid the many large boulders that would hang up the little outboard.

Slowly cruising the shore, we don't see any sign of oil. I get off on the boulders at the base of an avalanche track and poke around, but all is clean. Tiny meltwater rivulets trickle between, under and over the boulders. The sun is warm, and on a south facing slope I find early currant blooms. Leaving the shore, we cut across the lagoon to check the other side, and then make our way back out to the *Spirit*.

Harbor Air wings over as Mike and I climb aboard. The plane circles McCarty Lagoon several times, right over the area Mike and I had just checked from the Avon. The pilot radios Don that he sees a large patch of sheen and mousse on the water. I know it is clean and suspect he is seeing the detrital scum on the surface. How many times, how many places, is oil reported where there isn't any and missed where it is? In Prince William Sound, I saw and smelled oil on the water and beaches from about 50 feet in the air. But out here, after weathering a month and with scattered distribution, it is not so easy. The most reliable method of mapping oil is to walk the beaches, sometimes reaching down to flip the kelp or roll boulders. Harbor Air radios that they still can't pick up Karen and will be back in a couple hours.

Don takes the *Spirit* up the fjord to Desire Creek. The beach here is narrow and rocky. Karen and I walk the full length of it but find no evidence of oil. After returning to the *Spirit*, I take my book to a sheltered sunny nook on the upper deck. Across the fjord, Dinglestadt Glacier flows off the Harding Icefield in a narrow valley. The morainal spit by the ranger station curves out into the water. Early seagulls sweep and squawk around the minuscule gravel island where they nest. Bud has been tracking chick and nest counts on that island for several years, and the population is steadily increasing.

Lulled by the sun, I slip into sleep and my book drops to the deck. I am so tired and assaulted. My soul retreats to some small hidden place within me and draws a grey fog curtain around her. But the shroud is not enough to keep the dreams at bay. I rise and sink through the film of consciousness, yesterday's reality as horrifying as today's nightmares. Finally I rise, choosing activity to keep the dreams away over rest in the sun.

In late afternoon, a distant drone of a plane engine signals the return of the Harbor Air plane. It lands offshore from us, taxis toward shore and turns nose into the wind, waiting for us. Quickly, we load Karen, her gear and the precious specimens and samples into the Avon, and Randy ferries her over. My letter for Anne is stuffed in her pocket, along with my car keys. By now it is too late for Karen to catch a flight to Anchorage, and I do not want her to hitchhike the 125 miles to the city. Bud was supposed to be on this flight, and I watch the plane door eagerly, but Randy returns alone. The pilot brings word that Bud will be flown out the next morning. The engine turns over, and the plane is up on the step and airborne, climbing out over the fjord and curving east toward

Seward. Disappointed, I turn back into the cabin, and Randy and I begin supper preparations.

Soon afterward, Sandy, Jeff and Chuck return from their long day. They have done complete water quality, plankton, epibenthic sampling on the sea floor and fingerling seining at two locations today, and their work will continue long after dinner. I ask Don to take the *Spirit* back east along the coast to Paguna Arm of Two Arm Bay for the night. The weather continues calm and clear, and I want to get another early start tomorrow. Supper is suspended while we make the hour long run east along the outer coast in the sunset light.

The anchorage for the night is a slight indentation facing a short steep beach near the mouth of Paguna Arm. We finish fixing supper, and Sandy and Jeff are persuaded to leave their glass and cardboard box laboratory long enough to eat. After dinner, I take the Avon and row ashore in the last light. This area sank during the earthquake, leaving huge spruce with their roots inundated by salt water. Now the snags rise above the narrow beach, pebbles stacked steep around the trunks by winter storms. The tide is inbound, so I have to drag the Avon against the gradient and tie it securely to one of the snags. The light is nearly gone as I explore the shore, too dark to see if any oil is at my feet. I try to move inland to the small flat perched below bedrock cliffs, but become enmeshed in the tangle of drift logs and fallen snags, mantled with beach pebbles from mighty storm waves. Drawn by the sound of a large waterfall, my boots crunch through the pebbles to a stream. Following it over the berm, I find a quiet pool, fed by the tumbling waterfall. In the soft dark gathering around me, the waterfall spray seems to glow against the cliff rocks and the tumult of sound and cool mist envelops me. Behind me, *Spirit* gleams in the last light, her reflection checkered with cabin light. I linger a few minutes, slowing the racing of my mind. In the calmness, I find fragments of peace for my heart. I make my way back to the Avon and find it nearly afloat in the rising tide. The splash and drip of water off the oars is a delicate counterpoint to the waterfall and the lap of waves as I row back to the *Spirit*.

Sandy and Jeff are still hard at it as I brush my teeth at the deck railing and go below to my bilge berth. I had hoped to be sharing this night with Bud, and I feel his absence keenly. Again the nightmares chase through my sleep, tormenting me from rest. Sharp claws grab at my fragile grey fog shelter, ripping holes where black torrents pushed by the moon gush in and flood over me. Several times I surface from sleep, but the bilge is as dark as my dreams, and I hear no morning sounds signaling the return of the sun.

May 2

Finally the peeping of Randy's watch releases me. I dress quietly by the feel of my clothes and find the door out of the darkness. Quiet calm morning again, such a string of good weather after the stormy beginning. Groggily, I go through the morning routine, setting on water and coffee, brushing my teeth and hair. Such ordinary actions, set against the coming light of day in the midst of such extraordinary tasks. My heart rises with the sun on the peaks. Sometime this morning that blue and white plane should bring Bud to join us. When I take coffee up to Don, he teases me about clearing out the "Bridal Suite" for Bud and I. The coast and ship create a honeymoon of dreams, the task at hand draws a pall over those dreams. Today I plan to walk as many beaches as we can, surveying strand by strand for oil contact.

The Avon is dew wet as I step down with oars and ammo can seat. In the cool of the night, the pontoons got soft. I feel like their softness matches my energy as I row ashore to revisit the waterfall beach while the rest of the crew wake and breakfast. I walk the full length of the beach, checking for oil and possibilities as an outer coast ranger camp. No oil is located, but it looks like a good location for a camp on shore. A couple flat places, sheltered from ocean winds by the berm and brush, fresh water. Don is ready to move by the time I row back to the *Spirit*.

Slowly we cruise up the east shore of Paguna Arm. This is an enchanting fjord, with glaciers peering out of high valleys from the ice field, braided streams pouring grey silt water into the ocean, patches of spruce and alder painting the history of disturbance and substrate along the rocky walls. I decide to check the beach at the head of the fjord since it matches the beaches at the head of Taroka Arm which are so fouled by mousse. Sandy and I row the Avon ashore and walk the beach in both directions. Neither of us find any oil. So much for that theory of oil distribution. The winds and tides and currents are playing a large role in the final deposition of mousse. Reembarking, we turn south and follow the west side of the fjord.

During our inspection of the beaches, the long awaited message from the air taxi finally comes over the radio. They should arrive in a few minutes, and on this flight, Bud is aboard! Don turns on the loudspeaker, and orders "OK Chuck, clear out of the honeymoon suite for Bud and Page." I am too excited to even blush.

Soon I hear the plane from the east and watch it descend over the mountains and land near the *Spirit*. Spray arches away from the floats as it taxis to a stop, settling into the water off our bow. Randy is taxi man again and takes the Avon over to pick up Bud. It seems forever as they unload his gear and row back to the *Spirit*. His eyes are smiling as he gets closer. He boards and envelopes me in a hug. The back deck is crowded with all our gear and equipment and the whole crew. Soon it seems that everyone is talking at once, handing up Bud's gear. Bud brings our first news from town in several days, and he has not heard much from the coast since we've been gone. The work of the day is suspended while we catch up. Bud is excited to finally be out on the coast. It has been a couple weeks since his voyage with Bill and Anne, and much has changed in that time.

Karen made it into Seward all right last night, bringing the samples and my letter directly to Anne in the MAC meeting. Bud says that Anne started reading the letter to herself, then simply read the whole thing aloud to the MAC group. I hope that means that the list of beaches for cleanup will get immediate attention from the Coast Guard and EXXON. I feel strangely outside the world Bud is telling us about. The politics, the various agencies, the shifting, scrambling, conflicting and always changing activities in Seward and out the coast both east and west of us. My world has focused on the immediate tasks at hand: the mapping of the oil, the collection of samples, the documentation of impacts. The incredible tangle of logistics and tasks and weather and tides and people and equipment. The dawning realization of how large the task and how short the voyage. I really want a few minutes alone with Bud, but there doesn't seem to be an opportunity for that. Finally I decide to get on with the work of the day; there are many miles of coast to go, and the weather is cooperating. Chuck and I decide to check the beaches at the end of the west side of Paguna Arm, and Bud joins us in the Avon. Chuck goes in one direction, Bud and I in the other. On the steep pebble beach, I explain to Bud how we've been surveying: walking parallel lines along the kelp strands when there are two of us, or weaving between them when I'm alone. We find no tar balls in the pebbles, neither do we make a private connection after the days apart. Soon we join Chuck, who also reports clean beach, return to the *Spirit* and head on out the arm. Although I want to check some of the more exposed beaches, the surf is too high for landing. The inflatable operators are willing to take me to shore, but no one will join me on the beaches. Although the surf is gentle for this country, it is sure to drench me during landing or launching, and we bypass the rest of the beaches in Paguna Arm.

Out on the outer coast again, Don continues east toward Harris Bay. I really want to check an exposed beach, and finally in Cup Cove, we decide to try it. The surf is lower at the south end, and Sandy, Bud and I head in. It takes all three of us to carry the inflatable with the engine, anchor, oars and gear up the beach and secure it to a boulder near the cliff. Walking the sandy beach, we find several patches of tar balls melting into the kelp and sand. Already these tar patches are more spread out than those I saw two days ago, melting in the sun and spreading further and deeper into the surface layers of sand. At the north end of the beach, a waterfall arches off the cliff and over a shallow cave in the bedrock. The waves are breaking and running up the beach, alternately flooding and retreating from the entrance to the cave. Laughing and stumbling in my orange suit, I run into the cave between waves. Soon Sandy and Bud join me. Looking back out through the water veil, the *Spirit* is framed by rock walls and backdropped by islands and open sea. The beach stretches in front of us, three lines of human tracks wobbling its length in our search. Soon, the tide will smooth away our tracks, but the tar balls are not so easily erased.

We each run the water gauntlet out of the cave and head back to the Avon. River otter tracks litter the sand, some of them left since the outgoing tide. We can read their lives for the past day or two. Here two ran along the tideline, here there are several sets of tracks between water and woods homes. Piles of scat and urine called spraints are left in the sand or perched on rocks, often several deposits in the same place. The droppings show the diet of mussels and fish in the shards of shell and bone. The footprints show where they whirl and roll and slide in the sand, tracks intertwined with each other and the rocks and logs of their landscape. At the edge of the spruce, narrow otter trails pad gently through the deep mosses; one otter wide, indentations barely discernable to us, regular trails to otter noses. Often these shallow otter trails go over small passes between coves, a short cut for bad weather or busy days. Part of me explores their world with delight; surely in some other lifetime I was an otter. And my scientist part follows their tracks through the tar ball lines to the oiled sea and wonders what the impacts are on their food sources, and the food sources of those beings and on and on. I try to figure out how to estimate the current populations, where and how they move through the land, and how we can track their numbers in the generations to come into this changed place. Bud's shout breaks into my thoughts and I retrace my steps to meet Bud and Sandy at the Avon. Back to the *Spirit*, on to another set of beaches.

As we cruise up the coast, Bud gathers with the crew in the cabin, full of excited talk and stories. I stand at the edge of the group, unable to engage in the stories, unable to connect with him. He is fully a National Park Service ranger, uniformed, immersed in the oil spill activities, using all his knowledge and skills to Protect The Resource. But I cannot find my lover or companion of the land in this person. I go out to the upper deck and stand by the pilot house as we swing around Point Harris and up into the head of Harris Bay.

The tide is high and nearly covers the moraine that separates Harris Bay and Northwestern Lagoon. Although the chart shows only a depth of one fathom over the moraine, Don says he can take the *Spirit* into the lagoon through a break he knows in the moraine. The landmarks are his secret. And he barely slows down as we pass through the deepest part of the moraine. Last trip out here, the clouds were low and grounded icebergs were grey and blue in the cold evening light. This time the sun is high and bright on one of the most glorious fjords on the coast. Northwestern Lagoon has been very recently deglaciated with four tidewater glaciers still calving ice into the waters. Bedrock is bare and shiny grey around us, the forests in the valleys have the first generation of spruce trees in them. Don slows the *Spirit* and pulls in next to Long Beach on the eastern side of the lagoon. Mountains mantled with glaciers rise around us on three sides. When the tide is out, the lagoon is a lake, with a pouring outflow river in the break we just came through. When the tide is in, the moraine is covered with the sea, and the lagoon appears to be a long extension of Harris Bay. A brisk breeze ruffles the water's surface, causing sunlight glints off the wavelets and making the icebergs dance. The large ones are ponderous, moving to their own rhythm of melting, slowly rising and turning over as their equilibrium changes. Little ones jostle each other, tinkling like Christmas bells as they brush together. In the quiet after the engine is shut down, I hear profusions of birds celebrating spring and the end of their long migrations.

Rafts of sea otters float all along the moraine or dive and feed in the standing waves marking the lagoon entrance. Later Don tells us he counted 23 from one place. Several have very small pups on their chests. And one near the *Spirit* is massively pregnant. Usually an otter will swim away from us, watching down the length of her body and between her flippers. But this one has such a high belly, she can't see over herself. She has to turn her head from side to side to peer at us around her swollen body as she leisurely swims away. Her pup will be born soon, and I hope that she will stay back in this mountain magic place as the oil passes by the outer coast. In the days and weeks to come, the memory of her returns to me often to leaven my darkening dreams.

There are several long stretches of beach inside and outside Northwestern Lagoon. This is one of the treasures of the park, pristine scenery beyond description, critical wildlife habitats, important research opportunities emerging from the ice, hard won destination of kayakers and boaters. I split up the crew to survey the beaches and coves. Sandy, Chuck and Jeff unanimously take the west side beaches, leaving Bud and I alone to survey Long Beach. Quickly, we gather gear and lunch and are ferried to the west end of the beach. We have begun a ritual as each of us leaves the *Spirit* to walk a new beach. The person leaving is helped into the inflatable, willing hands holding the ladder and bow rope, handing down equipment, tossing the rope onto the floorboards. "Bye, good luck, hope you don't find anything. . . ."

Long Beach lives up to its name, an extension of the moraine across the lagoon left by the glacier when it began its retreat about 1910. The beach is nearly three miles long, curving around a complex pond and estuary system, fronting a tidal lagoon which fills and drains through a break in the beach wall at the far eastern end. This is one of the areas I located for further study while flying the seabird survey. If oil gets into the labyrinth between beach and cliffs, it will contaminate a large shallow area. Oil in exposed areas with a lot of pounding wave action will be removed or broken down more rapidly than oil deposits in these quiet backwaters with little energy.

Bud and I start following the kelp lines of recent tides around and among the boulders and sand patches. The sun is warm and brilliant, making me squint. Happily, I left the Mustang suit on board the *Spirit*, and I rejoice in the relative freedom of lighter clothes and knee boots. We follow the lagoon entrance along the width of the moraine, coming to the point where the beach juts into Harris Bay, then follows along the moraine to the east. Bud, ahead of me, shouts that he has found a dead bird. As I approach, he holds up a huge wing and long spindly leg. Remains of a sandhill crane, thrown about by scavengers and tide. We locate most of the pieces, both wings, legs, breastbone and head. There is no evidence of oil on the bones or feathers or nearby rocks so we don't collect it for evidence. We take photos for the record, and a couple feathers, and move east around the point.

Then up in the high tide line where the waterborne kelp is twisted around the old beach ryegrass roots, the shells seem to wink at me from the sand. I pause and rub my eyes, thinking that my lack of rest is catching up with me. Light glints at me from shiny black mussel shells. As I glance ahead, there are more flashes in the sun, sparkles decorating the tideline. When I kneel to examine them closer, I see the mussel shells filled with melted tar, brilliant shiny surface winking like faceted obsidian. The tar balls extend along the beach for several hundred feet.

At least this one is easy to collect. I simply slide shells full of oil into the jar. "Look Ma, clean hands!" We take our notes, the official photos, the official specimens, trying to describe in words and collect in microcosm this desecration. The documentation of oiled coast comes out as discreet items, somehow separating the system of the oil spill from the systems of the land. But the reality is that the one is overlaid on the other, and they are becoming woven together into a web that cannot be disentangled. I am beyond shock at finding this oil here. The knowledge sinks into me like a stone in cold mud, leaving no ripple, adding mass to the load in my spirit.

The surf is pounding as Bud and I walk down the length of Long Beach. Even on this calm day, the thundering waves are higher than my head and landing an inflatable here would result in swamping and a bath for all involved. Each wave arches white and foaming over the beach, then folds and crashes onto the granite cobbles. The froth drives upslope, catching my boots, then retreats back to the sea, dragging rocks in its teeth. The beach is made up of granite cobbles, almond to orange size, all smoothly rounded, mica bits flashing in the sun. The walking is difficult, and Bud slowly pulls ahead along the tideline. I move inland over the storm ridge to explore the estuary system behind the beach. Winter storm waves sweep over the beach, carrying loads of rocks and driftwood. The debris is deposited in the backwater area, some of it a quarter mile from the ocean.

This area is composed of sand and silt deposited by the outwash from the glacier. The wind blasts through the area, carving away sand and snow. Strange little islands covered with spruce rise ten to twenty feet above the estuary plain where the tree roots hold the soil against the wind. The trees are bent and stunted, tenaciously creating and holding the only high ground around. Melting drifts of gritty snow hunker down in the lee of the sand islands and the tree trunks. The landscape is a strange meshing of processes: aeolian, glacial, and tidal. I wander solitary through this scape of coming spring. The maze of brackish water channels weaves through the islands and lower rises of beach ryegrass-covered sand dunes. Flotsam abandoned by higher tides is scattered about. I find an old boat, driven ashore in a winter storm, on her side in the driftwood and half filled with sand. Her bright yellow paint catches my eye in the sand and granite cobbles. Fat chubby tugboat, it fits in my hand, some child's toy lost overboard or taken by the rising tide. I take it for Don to add to his fleet of Kenai Fjords Tour boats.

I explore most of the estuary zone behind the beach, making my way over to the stream draining the valley between bedrock walls. The sun is warm, and I hope to find some fresh water for a quick bandanna bath, but the tide is rising and the breeze is brisk. Squinting into the sun, I see Bud cresting the beach ridge down by the outlet stream, heading back from his survey of the main beach. I work my way south through the maze of tidal channels and ponds overlaid with a filigree of goose tracks. None too soon, as the tide is coming in and the channels are filling deeper than my boots. We meet for lunch in the lee of the beach ridge. The sun is warm as we spread out our raingear and nest down in the winter-dried beach ryegrass next to a huge battered drift log. We dig into our packs for bread and cheese and oranges. We find a few quiet minutes together, surrounded by mountains and sun, the roar of surf behind us. Our talk is local: surf conditions; feasibility of getting an inflatable into the estuary through the outlet stream; the importance of the estuary to birds and wildlife and fish; glacial formation of the beach. Neither of us has found any more oil. Tentatively, we look ahead to a time beyond the madness, perhaps a kayak trip here in summer. Maybe--if the area doesn't get oiled in the weeks ahead. Wearily, we sit propped against the trunk with our arms around each other. The wind curls over the log and ruffles the top of my hair. The warmth of the sun teases the scent out of the dry grass, pungent and salty and a little dusty. Then the radio squawks, and someone is asking our location and plans. I find the radio under my pack and tell them we're at the far end of the beach and will be back in an hour. Then I remember we have a three-mile walk back through loose cobbles.

 Reluctantly, we stuff gear and clothes back in our packs and start down the beach. The walking is a little easier on the back side of the beach ridge. Alternate stripes of beach ryegrass in the sand, and places where the waves breached the beach ridge and threw down their loads of shells and granite rocks. I pick up one of the cobbles, and it lays in my palm; white, with flecks of mica catching the sun. I take it back with me, one clean reminder among the oily samples.

Back aboard the *Spirit*, Don maneuvers her through the thickening pack of icebergs toward the array of glaciers cascading off the icefield and into the ocean. Reflections double the beauty around us, every iceberg has a mirror, floating in reflections of glaciers and mountains, distorted by our bow wave. We are pretty well surrounded with ice when we are abreast the south side of Striation Island. No harbor seals in sight, even though we scan the ice ahead with binoculars. Sandy and Jeff make a quick plankton haul and collect water samples off the bow.

One of the joys of this trip is that every observation, every collection, every description, adds to our knowledge of this coast. Prior to the oil spill, very little data had been collected for the outer coast, especially for the non-summer seasons. Even as we are documenting oil spread and effects, we are also building the baseline knowledge of this system. This opportunity to work with scientists from different fields is a pleasure to me and helps me build an integrated understanding of the land and the processes which shape her.

Shadows begin to accumulate in the crevasses of ice and behind the mountains and icebergs around us. Off our bow, Anchor and Ogive Glaciers pour steeply over the mountain, spawning fractured ice. The land is a study of blue and white--shadows, ice, water, sky, clouds, snow--punctuated by patches of grey bedrock. Deep glacial ice captures the sunlight, reflecting the short visible wavelengths in a pure delicate blue, touched by a tint of green, frosted by blinding white. This is a color only achieved by live light and old ice. To the east of us, Striation Island rises vertical and barren from the silty fjord waters. It is very recently exposed from the ice, with no cushioning layer of soil, and no nearby source of seeds. The park staff maintains a photo point on top of it to track the current movements of the glaciers at the head of the lagoon.

Too soon Sandy finishes his collections, and Don turns our stern to the glaciers and heads back out to the cut in the moraine. As the *Spirit* moves outbay, we approach a large flat iceberg with dark spots all over it. At first, I suspect the harbor seals have materialized and are basking in the sun. But the objects turn out to be ten sea otters hauled out on the ice and very reluctant to take to the water. Their fur is dried soft and light, almost a sheen of gold over normally wet dark fur. Conventional wisdom maintains that sea otters very seldom leave the water, perhaps seeking the rocks only in the midst of severe winter storms. But on this trip we have seen otters on rocks and ice on several occasions, and none of them seem to be suffering for it. As the *Spirit* passes by, one by one they slip over the edge of the ice and pop their heads back up to watch our progress.

Shadows are stretching across Harris Bay as we leave Northwestern Lagoon. There is one more long rocky beach on the west side of Harris Bay I want to check before we call it a day. The beach is over two miles long, reaching from a valley with another hidden lake north almost to the moraine heading Harris Bay. A tall bedrock sea mount breaks the beach at the midpoint. Vertical bedrock pillar carved out by the glaciers, plunging into the sea on one side, pinning the beach to the mountain on the other. Chuck and Jeff take the north side; Bud and I head south. Mountains already hide the sun from us as we start down the beach. We follow along the recent tidelines full of torn kelp. Bud finds one tar ball, melting shiny black over the rocks and into the substrate.

As Bud and I start back, I become aware of the screeching screams of bald eagles. A pair of eagles alternately circles and lands near a large nest in a tall old spruce. This is the first pair I have seen near a nest this year. The neighborhood has changed since they left last fall. I wonder how they will fare this summer as they lay and hatch eggs and raise and fledge chicks. Bud goes into the old growth to see if the eagles are bringing oiled carrion back to the nest for feeding. The eagles keep a wary eye on both of us, but don't leave the nest tree while Bud checks the ground below them. He reports lots of droppings and old fish bones, but nothing recent on the ground. The eyrie itself is a huge cupped platform of sticks, grass, rope, feathers, old bones and eagle droppings. A pair of eagles will reuse nests, often rotating between two or three over several years. Maybe the nest needs a season or two to air out after raising one to three messy eaglets. The adult eagles send us on our way with a chorus of hoarse screams.

I watch the beach rocks carefully, hoping to find an eagle feather among the tidal flotsam. Eagle feathers are a symbol of the sacred to me, and after this day of sporadic oil and incredible mountain beauty, I would like to see one. Not to keep, just to hold for a few minutes. I love the long dark curving shape of the pinions, the softness of the barbs carved by the speed of the wind. But the eagles appear to be keeping their feathers for now, and seagull feathers just don't have the same effect.

The last sunlight glows on the mountains across the bay as we return to the landing place and Randy comes for us in the Zodiac. We have another calm night in the forecast, so Don agrees to anchoring in Taz Basin. It is a short run down from Harris Bay, half way along the west side of Granite Island. It seemed a tight squeeze when Eric took the *Shaman* into Taz Basin on the previous trip. The *Spirit* is even larger, but we head right for the narrow entrance in the rocks and slip into quiet waters. Don anchors up for the night at the south end. The snow level has retreated up the cliffs, but the waterfalls continue unabated. The grey bedrock walls rise vertical all around us, enfolding this tiny pocket of water and our vessel. Tonight others take over supper responsibilities. I go through notes and maps, copying the daily litany of beaches onto a duplicate set of maps. When I finish, I take a mug of wine up to the upper deck and rest surrounded by rock and water, watching the last light fade away overhead. Mike brought his saxophone, and tonight he gets it out, playing blues on the deck below me. The music rises, echoing and reverberating around the granite concert hall. The melodies are wound about with the music of falling water, and quiet percussion from slapping of tiny waves along the hull. The peace of the basin steals over me as I wait for supper in the gathering chill of evening. I feel the quiet satisfaction of much work accomplished and the companionship of the team. It is good to have Bud out here to share the work with me. I am heartened that Harris Bay and Northwestern Lagoon have so far largely escaped oiling, and rejoice at all the otters and birds and bear tracks I have seen today.

Don has checked the water supply and tells us that we have been so careful using water that there is enough for short showers all around! After supper, I take my turn in the narrow shower. The warm water is an incredible luxury. Clean and tired, I snuggle up beside Bud in the privacy of the "honeymoon cabin." Bud's body smells like the salty sun-warm beach ryegrass, and I fall asleep with his arms around me and the murmur of waves on the hull. Tonight the nightmares are not so rampant.

May 3

This morning I wake up from hearing Randy stirring in the bilge. He has the coffee and water pots on by the time I stumble into the cabin. The morning is grey and cold; clouds have moved in during the night. Bud joins Don and I for our morning watch. Daylight accumulates above the rim of our chamber, gradually bringing substance to the trees, rocks and waterfalls. A slight swell makes its way into the entrance, barely rippling the surface of the water in the basin.

Soon the whole crew is awake. Don and Randy hoist the anchor, and we are on our way while everyone is still finishing breakfast. This is the last full day of our voyage, and we need to cover all of Aialik Bay before nightfall. The east side of the Aialik Peninsula and Bear Glacier Beach can be reached in day trips from Seward, so I leave those areas for later in the week. *Spirit* slips out of the basin entrance, facing the wind and swells of the Gulf of Alaska. The grayness of the day holds my weariness close to me. I watch constantly for oil, whales, sea lions and otters as we go around Granite Cape, across Granite Passage, and head north up the west shore of Aialik Bay.

I have heard rumors of oil reported in Verdant Cove, so we start the day's patrol work there. Bud is also concerned because there is a historic site in the cove, and on his earlier trip he saw an unauthorized camp or equipment dump onshore there. Bud, Chuck and I go ashore at the east end of the beach and start following the kelp lines. Almost immediately, we find thick tar balls caught in the kelp and thrown on the shore by high tides. Although today is cold and misty, the tar has melted and oozed through the kelp and into the pebbles. As the tar melts and flows down, it radiates out, covering a larger and larger area in the lower layers of rocks. Already, there is melted and congealed mousse six inches into the beach. When I pick up the kelp, the tar and decomposing vegetation drips black slime. It smells foul, slightly petroleum scented and rotten. The oiled kelp line extends around the curve of the beach. We find three disintegrating bird carcasses. Bud and Chuck tentatively identify them as pigeon guillemonts, but it is hard to tell. I collect a sample of the oil for the investigators, and Bud rolls the birds into a garbage sack to take with us. We find signs of a recent camp and fire, but the equipment has been removed. I knock down a driftwood shelter frame at the camp site and scatter the half burned-logs.

Then we skip up the side of Aialik Bay and take the Avon to spot check the long beach outside Pederson Lagoon. Our first stop is inside the curve of the beach. Light misty fog shrouds the land. Delicate water drops have condensed on the grasses and spruce needles, and in our hair and the men's beards. Several eagles are in the dead spruce back of the beach, but we see no sign of a nest. However the spruce are splattered with white droppings, and it appears to be a popular place. I wander around the bases of the trees to check for any carrion which may have been brought over and dropped. Nothing but old fish bones. But I do find a small eagle feather caught in the brown grasses. The mist has condensed on the surface, beading it with transparent pearls against the dove grey of the barbs. It is beautiful. The loan of this feather feels like a gift to me, a reassurance that the land will heal and function again. A soothing to my deep grief. Carefully, I carry the feather to the Avon and leave it on the pontoon to show Bud when he returns. He is back before I return again, and not pleased that I brought the feather from its resting place. I am stunned. Inside that Mustang suit is the uniform of a ranger who knows that federal law prohibits non-Native people from owning eagle feathers. He wants nothing to do with the feather, even temporarily. I leave the feather gently under one of the eagle roosts, laying it down so as not to disturb the mistfall.

We work our way up the beach, stopping at several more locations south of the entrance, then continuing on to the north beach. Several more sites are checked, but there is no sign of oil, and we are getting further and further upbay. The fog thickens and icebergs start to crowd our Avon. They can be razor sharp, and the inflatable is not as durable in ice as old *Tin Lizzy*. After checking over two and a half miles of beach, I call it clean and we return to the *Spirit*.

We have a hot lunch while Don takes the *Spirit* south and up inside Holgate Arm. This is a major destination for the Kenai Fjords Tours in the summer. They take the tour boats right up to Holgate Glacier, surrounded by brash ice. Holgate is a very active tidewater glacier, pouring down a narrow valley off the Harding Icefield. While we are checking the beaches, Don takes the *Spirit* up the arm to check on the glacier, to see how it fared over winter. But he only makes it inside the first headland before the ice is too thick and he returns to meet us.

I want to check the beaches between Holgate and Verdant Cove to find how far up the fjord the oil has come. The foggy solitude feels good to me as I walk the beaches. Back in foul weather gear of layers of polypropylene and bunting, hip boots and zipped up in the Mustang suit. There is an invincible feeling that comes from being warm and dry in nasty weather. I splash across streams with aplomb and crunch along the pebble beaches. In contrast to yesterday's sunny blue and white world, today is full of greys: light dirty snow, grey rocks, steel grey water, white icebergs, green-black spruce and fog over everything. We pull into Quicksand Cove and row ashore to the beach. This time we find human footprints tangled in with the land otter and crow and raven tracks, but neither oil nor carcasses stranded in the tideline. Bud and I explore the mature old spruce stands at either end of the beach. Driftwood, sand and shells are thrown hundreds of feet into these woods by winter storms. We are concerned that these storms will resuspend and carry oil way up into the terrestrial ecosystems during winter. And that huge pounding waves will bury oil deep in the gravel of the beach.

The next beach is on the south shore of McMullen Cove. The cove curves to the south like a comma. Our family ducked in here twenty years ago during a sailing trip to Aialik Bay. I remember a dark and stormy night when we looked for a camping place ashore in the pouring rain. We found nothing but dripping black spruce and wet driftwood looming over the short beach. The land is still dark and wet, the beach steep and rocky. This time though, we go ashore to walk our tideline. Bud and I slip and stumble over the wet algae-covered rocks, looking for the tidal debris marking tideline among the crevices of the rocks. Startled, we crouch over the matted green algae and drift sticks. A flaky white substance is sprinkled over the dark slimy surface. It looks like Ivory Snow soap flakes. It melts and smears on our fingers at body temperature. And lifted to our noses, it smells strongly of gasoline. Puzzled, we collect a sample for identification. It is definitely a foreign material on these shores, but whether it is a derivative of the crude, a dispersant or cleaning agent, or something unrelated to the oil spill is hard to tell. EXXON repeatedly maintains that they are not using or testing dispersants, but rumors keep surfacing of low flying planes spraying the water. We scramble on around the beach curve, trying to check the tideline between the boulders. Happily, we don't find any oil or carcasses.

Don heads the *Spirit* east across Aialik Bay. I want to check at least one beach on the east side, trying to pin down the pattern of oil distribution on both sides of the fjord. The sky becomes darker with evening, clouds lowering even further, slipping down the mountain sides. Weather is coming in and our days of grace are over. Lucky we're headed back to town tomorrow. It is too much work to get out of my Mustang suit and back in again on the other side of the bay. So after selecting Ranger Beach off the chart, I go up to the bow and snuggle in just under the railing. I'm braced between the low railing and the anchor winch, rolling with the waves. A stiff breeze blows across the bow, and a fine mist is settling over the bay. With hands pushed up in my sleeves muff-style and the hood over my head, I'm perfectly warm and content. Like a sea otter on her back in the swells, anchored by a strand of kelp, the rhythm of the sea lulls me to sleep. I awake when Don reduces power in front of my chosen beach. Bud, Mike and I go ashore on Ranger Beach. In sunny weather, this beach has a gorgeous view up Holgate Arm and Aialik Bay. But now it is drippy and bleak. Quickly, we walk the length of the beach without finding any evidence of oil in the pebbles.

It is getting seriously gloomy as Don takes *Spirit* up the coast to Tooth Cove and anchors her near the stream and beach at the head. Rain begins in earnest as we begin supper preparations in the cozy womb of the cabin. Looking out of the pilot house, Don remarks that the cove looks like the Aleutians on a good day. It is a grey and black world, narrowly defined by steep snowy mountains slopes, cut with black avalanche gashes. The clouds lower down into the mountain ring above us. We float between steel water and grey sky, with a thin filling of snow and rocks around us. Jeff takes it into his head to try for a halibut and ignores the derisive comments of the crew about his chances. Standing on the back deck, he patiently works the jig, rain running off his raingear, hands turning red from wind and cold. Occasionally, someone looks out and remarks on his obvious lack of intelligence and halibut savvy. Suddenly the rod jerks in his hand. The peanut gallery dismisses it as a rock. Then: "Oh, maybe it is a halibut. It *is* a halibut!" A stampede for the aft deck, lots of coaching and advice. "Give it line! Reel it in!

Let it out! Get the net! Hey, it's a big one!" Finally Randy nets it and swings it thumping onboard. A good twenty pounds of fresh halibut thrashes in our gear until it is killed with a blow to the head. Randy and I clean and fillet it while supper finishes cooking. Then we make up a pan full of fillets to bake with mayonnaise and lemon slices. Tonight dessert is fresh halibut, and most of us have seconds.

Night wraps our deep narrow cove in darkness as we finish supper and clean up the galley. I am feeling the relief of a big job nearly finished. Ranger Beach was our last on this trip. Tomorrow morning we will head straight for Seward. We have walked 62 separate beaches, all in the park. Eighteen of these are oiled to varying degrees. We have collected samples, photographs and notes documenting the spreading pestilence. We have explored incredible country and walked in lands and seasons new to scientists. Breathtaking pristine landscapes, ringed by a narrow strangling cord of tar.

I start to realize how weary I am, sitting at the fogged windows with a cup of tea, watching the rain blast the panes and run down the gutters. This survey is only the first round of monitoring the oil impacts and trying to figure out the best places and times and ways to clean it. The job will go on and on, through the summer, into fall, in the winter if weather permits, then back in the spring. I have walked 44 of the beaches, coordinated all the logistics for the crews, attempted to integrate oiling locations with wind and water currents, tides, topography and timing. I look forward to sleeping late in the morning while we get underway, to reporting back to Anne on our work, even to dealing with the investigators and turning over our samples and maps and notes. Then a few days off. A desperately needed break to get away from the frenzy, tend to business in Anchorage, move into Bud's new house. And most of all, to sleep. During this voyage, I have come to know that this work will continue for months, and that we must each learn how to live in it and take care of ourselves. I turn away from the window and go below to join

Bud in our little cabin. We turn off the light and snuggle together, falling asleep immediately.

May 4

We ignore the peeping of Bud's watch alarm. Soon others get up. Half awake, mostly asleep, I monitor their progress through morning rituals of getting dressed, brushing teeth, fixing breakfast in the galley. The small patch of the world we can see through the porthole is grey and drizzly, no welcome invitation to jump up and start the day. I had hoped to sleep in this morning, catching up on much needed rest before we land in Seward. But it is after eight, and we are still at anchor. Soon there are footsteps outside our door, then a hesitant knocking. "What's the plan, Boss?" We are already out of bed and half dressed. I repeat instructions of last night for our travels. "Straight into Seward, weather permitting." We layer on warm clothes against the cold rain outside and emerge into the main cabin. Hot water and coffee are already steaming on the stove. A simple trip above decks to the pilot house requires full raingear and boots. We gather behind Don as he powers up *Spirit's* engines and turns her bow out into Aialik Bay. The seas are fairly calm, and the windshield wipers slap back and forth as we head south towards Aialik Cape.

One by one the crenelated coves of the Aialik Peninsula slip by. From the air this is incredible country, a delicate lacework of land stringing out into the Gulf. Wrinkled and twisted, just the tops of marine mountains rising above the ocean. In many places there are narrow mountain passes several hundred yards wide between Resurrection and Aialik Bays. But the same destination by boat means a trip of 50 miles around Aialik Cape and back up the coast again.

The weather looks little changed since that night twenty years ago of the ill-fated exploration of McMullen Cove. Finding no place to camp ashore, Dad rigged a tarp over the cockpit of *Sailboat* and headed across Aialik Bay. Rain poured off the tarp and down Mom's sleeve as she held it against the wind. We found an anchorage and campsite in one of these bays. We hunkered down in leaky tents and steadily dampening sleeping bags beneath the dripping spruce. The next morning I watched Dad the first and only time I have ever seen him start a fire with fuel. This was before the days of lightweight backpacking stoves, and we needed a fire for warmth and cooking and an attempt to dry our gear. We tried to buck around Aialik Cape, but the seas were too high for our little vessel, and we retreated back to the beach at the head of the cove. All day we kept the fire going, explored our tiny beach and played checkers on top of the grubbox with pebble and shell markers. We had met seal hunters up by Aialik Glacier who had given us seal liver and hearts. This was our dinner, and I never had liver so good.

The next day we struck camp again and loaded *Sailboat* for another attempt on the cape. Again the seas tossed us about, and we ran for shelter in Paradise Cove at the back of Three Hole Bay. Here we found two huge crabbing vessels who had also hidden from the storm. Happily we rafted alongside them, *Sailboat* looking like a tiny dingy next to their bulk. Their anchor lines reached clear to the bottom of the deep cove, and their decks provided a place for energetic children to play. Their cook made us hot oatmeal with fruit cocktail. That night I slept in their hold on a huge coil of rope. The sky finally cleared the following day and we went our separate ways. Dad and I took *Sailboat* around the cape while Mom, John, Lynn and Bill hiked over the pass from Chat Cove. The swells were still monstrous, and the barrel of fish and glacier ice overturned in the engine, killing it. We bobbed in sudden silence, watching the surf pound the vertical cliffs. The engine caught and started on the first pull, an absolute first. Then we made our way around into the cove to pick up the rest of the crew. We had many more adventures before finally arriving back in Seward.

Now as I watch the coast passing in the rain from the dry pilot house, I remember that earlier trip. At least this time I'm warm and dry, but this trip has cost me an innocence that carried me through scary and cold times before. Over the past 20 years this land has changed before my eyes--huge changes in half the span of my life. The sea otters have come again to these waters, recovering their numbers from the exploitation of the fur trade, but now they face an uncertain future. The land is besieged on all sides with development pressures. Several companies want to bring in huge cranes and pluck icebergs streaming from the water at the very face of the tidewater glaciers. Others want to build "wilderness lodges" on these shores, or hatcheries, or log the capes or mine the valleys. And now there is the pummeling from the oil creeping along the shore, insidiously floating into protected coves and nooks, lodging on rocks and logs and mussels. The associated invasion of humans and machinery and technology to "clean up" the uncleanable.

As we approach the bustle of the Seward boat harbor, the *Spirit* looks more like a successful salvage vessel than a tour boat. The Zodiac hangs off the side from the davits, the Avon is tied across the stern. The aft deck is heaped with equipment, garbage cans, trash we've collected, old floats, Mustang suits, outboard engines and fuel cans. After we are inside Caine's Head, each of us is busy packing gear and the extra food, equipment and samples. Sandy has coolers full of jars containing water, oil and plankton. Before we know it we're reducing speed and slipping between the breakwaters into the small boat harbor. We have not been in much floating mousse and the hull is still clean. Don has radioed ahead to the park office and Anne is on the dock to meet us. As the *Spirit* comes alongside, we jump down to make her fast.

Again Anne welcomes us home with hugs. Again we are thrust into the pandemonium of Seward, even busier than a month ago. Pickups are brought down and we rapidly unload all the boxes of gear and our precious specimens. Each of us is legally responsible for the collections we have made, and we keep a close eye on our respective bundles of samples. The investigators hover nearby, unwilling to let us out of their sight before they get their precious interviews.

We shanghai them to help with unloading. Sandy is anxious to start for Anchorage to see his new baby son so he gets first turn with the investigators.

As Anne and I walk up the dock after unloading the *Spirit* she says she is getting tired and has been grumpy with the park staff. No small wonder . . . She has been the political focal point for the National Park Service in Seward. As the realization sank in that oil would hit the shores of Kenai Fjords National Park, Anne assumed major responsibilities for coordinating and implementing the work of the Park Service. Originally, the National Park Service was the primary federal agency in Seward concerned with the oil spill. She was named leader of the MAC and has also been serving as Incident Commander for the past two or three weeks after the ICT left. Oh yes--and she is also the Superintendent of the park and the single Mom of three young daughters. Somehow in the quicksand of the shifting politics, players and weather-pushed oil, she keeps her head above water and a generally sunny, if somewhat frantic, disposition. She has been incredible throughout the crisis, keeping the needs of the land and the people before the ponderous bureaucracy, fostering a spirit of working together rather than EXXON-bashing. The toll of the stress is telling on her, as it is on all of us.

This return I manage to keep my equilibrium during the transition. The investigators are better organized and we know what to expect. Swiftly, they interview each of us, collect copies of notes, originals of maps, the samples we bring from the outer coast. Each piece of data has a number, a description, a date. But it is difficult to hand over the emotions of a beach full of tar with one sample jar. The tally of oiled miles and blackened carcasses omits the bear tracks following the tideline and the land otter humping out of the ocean over greased rocks to her lake hideaway. The dates and locations of our journey leave out the rain on our faces and the williwaws in the night and the blazing sun on the icebergs. Grimy and tired, I go over our trip with the investigator. "Just the facts, Ma'am."

I find a vacant phone and call Mom and Dad. I have had no word of Mom's condition since I left on the trip. She is at home, sounding tired but cheerful. Mom always sounds cheerful. During the week she has developed blood clots as a result of the hip surgery. Her physicians have tried to dissolve them by giving her medication to thin her blood and keep it from coagulating. As a result, she bleeds profusely with every little scratch or bruise. Even this is not enough, and they want her to return to the hospital. And she definitely does not want to go back. When she asks my opinion about her actions, I tell her that I think she should make her own choices about her health care. Get as much information as she needs and decide what is best for herself. And if these choices have serious consequences, then I will be sad, but I support her right to make those choices. I am shaken when I hang up the phone, wondering what the next hours and days will bring, how these decisions will play out. I wonder if I will see my Mom alive again.

Later I stop by Anne's office to check in with her. Looking up with a smile, she tells me she is trying to arrange the schedule so we can each have one day off over the weekend. I feel the walls close in around me. While on the trip, I had come to know that I need a minimum of three days off. A little time to be in a clean place with Bud, a trip to Anchorage to see Mom and get clothes for spring, time to run the multitude of errands that seem to be necessary in this society. I stammer that I had planned to take three days off from the oil spill work. Anne looks annoyed, but okays it *only* if I complete my trip report before Monday. I resolve that I will finish that report if I have to stay at the computer all night.

My chest is tight, and it is hard to breath as I step out into the street in front of the park office. Back bare hours and the stress closes over me like a vise. Without my knowledge, tears begin to stream down my face, and I stand bewildered. Then like a wounded animal, I frantically look for a place to hide. I find myself huddled in the lee of some summer shop buildings above the small boat harbor. The tears are cold on my face in the wind. Gradually, I sense someone nearby, and looking up I see Bill, the skipper of the park's boat. Awkward and concerned, he stands there: "Are you OK Page?" "No, I'm not." "Did you and Bud have a fight?" "No," the thought brings a smile through the tears. "I just can't do this anymore. I need a break. Just a few days to get centered again." Quietly he talks with me, neither expecting or getting answers. He talks about boats and the sea, and flying and supercubs and mountains and polar bears. The words do not matter, just his caring presence helps steady me. The crying dies away to a whimper and I wipe my eyes on my sleeves. Finally we both notice that we are shivering in the cold wind and he helps me to my feet. Then we turn to our interrupted tasks.

The Injury Assessment Center has been set up in the A-frame across the street from the park office. True, it still smells winter musty. But a couple tables and a row of folding chairs have been moved in. And phones are promised any day now. . . . A young college student, Peter Paul, has been hired to be the keeper of the supplies and equipment that are accumulating for the oil spill activities. He and I are the sole denizens of the A-frame. There is room to clean and repair equipment between trips, room for scientists to work, room for rangers to crash for the night and get a shower. Soon it will fill with Park Service and visiting scientists, and coast rangers during their breaks. The walls and floor and windows are bare, and the sound of our voices and steps rebounds noisily around the room. This definitely doesn't compare with the carpeted offices that EXXON is setting up downtown, but it looks like a palace to me. Now if I can just find my files and materials and retrieve the computer I was promised before I left.

During the move, everything someone thought might belong to me was piled in corners or in boxes. Some of it is outright junk, some of it belongs to the park, some of it is critical papers. We are beginning to be deluged with reports, papers, requests, paper, paper, paper. The oil spill has discovered the fax. When mated with the copy machine, an avalanche of important and trivial and even worthless material sweeps over us. Unfortunately, other crucial papers, photos and phone numbers have vanished during the week I was gone. Some of them surface days or weeks later, some never appear.

The matter of the computer is sticky. One of the early workers on the ICT left his computer for my use when he returned to Anchorage. Then the investigators needed it because their work mushroomed beyond any original expectations. But now we both need it. And they think possession is nine tenths of the law. Finally we reach agreement, and I can claim it the next day. For some reason, we can request nearly anything and have it shipped without problem. But our requests for computers are suspect. I don't care where they come from, but we cannot possibly implement a program of this magnitude and complexity without automation. We finally strip the Regional Office and other parks of all surplus and some necessary microcomputers to keep us going.

Late in the afternoon Bud and I both attend the Resources MAC meeting. The emphasis has changed direction to providing the regular MAC with information about the land and its resources and recommendations for shore cleanup. EXXON will be bringing a Shoreline Cleanup Assessment Team (SCAT) to Seward to check the beaches. They are to assess the contamination of each beach and evaluate how best to clean it up. The land managers in the Seward Zone want representatives to accompany them. And much of the land here is in the park. Bud and I both are put on standby to go with the SCAT team when they fly.

EXXON has not yet started cleaning up the list of beaches I sent in to Anne in the note. The Coast Guard has determined that they are to clean all the beaches at once, rather than getting to them one at a time. The result is that they spend time accumulating crews and boats, rather than getting out to the beaches. I am dismayed. Every day the sun shines, the tide rises, the tar balls melt and disperse deeper and further. Somehow my maps didn't make it to the Coast Guard. I xerox copies of the quads for the Coast Guard and VECO and remark them.

Then we get into a big discussion with ADEC about their oiling scale. They are reporting beaches as clean that Bud and I know are oiled. For starters, they only land their helicopter on beaches where they can get in above the high tide line. This means that they cannot access many of the steep beaches by cliffs. They extend the scale they were using in Prince William Sound, calculating oil impact in percent of beach covered between high and low tides. According to this system, 80-100% is heavy, 50-80% is moderate, 20-50% is light, and less than 20% is unoiled. This is frustrating, because their data make it seem as though the Seward zone has little to no oil on most of its beaches. The media and EXXON and the government act as though the oil stopped at Montague Straits and never left Prince William Sound. Finally Bud bursts out, "It may seem like no oiling to you, compared with Prince William Sound. But you must understand that a month ago this land was pristine." And that is the crux of the matter--this is not an issue of relativity.

Later ADEC revises their scale to describe the oiling as length and width and intensity of oiled area. This meshes with the data we collected and allows us to calibrate our intensive beach walking with their extensive fly overs. The bottom line is that they can track large areas and major oiling day to day. But often the insidious oiling in the kelp lines cannot be seen from the air. Sooner or later, you have to walk the beaches to nail down the extent of oiling. ADEC also asks that Bud and I fly with them, so one of us can compare both methods. Both ADEC and SCAT fly at low tide, weather permitting. So Bud and I take turns being ready to fly at a moment's notice.

It is getting late when Bud and I make our way home. All afternoon, showers and clean clothes and rest have seemed like a mirage. Now we luxuriate in the hot water sluicing away sweat and grime. All my clothes are sorted in piles for the washing machine, and I borrow clothes from Bud for the evening. We are too tired to wrestle with cooking, so decide to go to our friend Yvan's restaurant for supper. They have closed the kitchen by the time we get there, but the cook, Jean Marc, fires up the stove and makes us a wonderful dinner of fresh halibut with dill sauce. We eat slowly, savoring the food and company. Yvan is working like a madman: diving to check equipment, finishing construction on his apartments and dining hall, baking bread. But he takes time to sit and talk with us, bringing us back to reality with his jokes and hugs and deep understanding of the human foibles invading Seward. He is outrageous at times, and people at the ICT keep asking us if he is for real.

We return home, full and tired. From the porch, we look across the valley to Mt. Marathon, shadowed as the sun sets behind it. Last year, we climbed into the upper bowl with two friends and left a web of telemark turns down its little glacier. From this porch, we admired our tracks for days. Now our skis are rusting in the garage, and we probably would be out of breath just climbing the mountain.

I attempt to talk to Bud about my tears today. They start again as I try to explain how I feel, try to talk my way into an understanding of what is happening to me. But he cannot connect with me. Helplessly, he tries to hold me, my body shaking. "Are you OK honey?" "No, I just can't do this anymore. I need a break." "Do you want to see a doctor?" I know the medical profession cannot deal with this. I feel all disconnected. My mind and body and emotions are in separate discontinuous boxes. And most important of all, my spirit has become disconnected from the land. I have always felt a strong physical bond with the land. It runs through my back, down my legs and from my feet deep into the core of the earth. But that bond has become severed and I don't have that nurturing certainty. Now I feel the staggering, recoiling, reeling surges as the toxins pour down the energy pathways along the coastal currents with the tide and wind. I can't get my feet in the ground. I'm pushed and shoved around by every crisis, with no sense of priority or perspective. Desperately, I need to walk the mountains, sit in the stillness and feel the sun warm on my face, talk and cry and be held, and talk and talk some more. Bud is bewildered, and probably scared. His new wife is acting very strange, and he is overwhelmed with his own work. The evening springlight and smells of new earth and meltwater come through the open window over our heads. The nightmares chase me through the night again, playing with my mind, dangling my heart over abysses, catching my feet in immutable mud, silencing my screams.

May 5

Spring mornings are such a magic time. The newness of the season and the beginning of the day, all at once. This is a time for playing hookey, running off with the wild creeks and exploring their emerging banks and pools. A time to come home with wet feet, turning footwear into "swamp socks," never to be white again. We watch the ice go isothermal and rot into the stream in long slivers. Ducks are resting in the still ponds. The moose are rangy and scruffy, cows bulging with the last weeks of pregnancy before the birth of spindly red calves. Last year's cranberries melt out, soft and sweet from winter.

But I face this new spring morning exhausted. There is no hookey for me today. I pull on my clothes still warm from the dryer. A cup of hot chocolate, and I'm off to the office. The day begins with an ICT meeting. A swirl of information and logistics assaults us. Although we try to keep it short and concise, there is much to cover. We don't have time to discuss what we saw on the trip, only planning for the next voyages and dealing with the crises of the day. At least the ones we know about.

The VIP's have discovered the oil spill. There is a steady parade of people coming through who need to see the situation first hand. Congresspeople and staff, state officials, federal officials, special interest groups, the press. Anne does her best to arrange logistics so that they can dovetail with our work. But the visitors tend to be on fasttrack schedules. Leave Cordova in the morning, fly to Seward via Prince William Sound. Lunch in Seward, boat out to the outer coast in the afternoon and be in Kodiak by supper. The sheer distance makes this nearly impossible, and the weather is not cooperative. Tours of the oil spill become a scavenger hunt, with the prize going to whoever is on the dock when the weather breaks.

The scavenger hunt for ADEC and the SCAT crews revolves around flyable weather during low tides. We have to have a National Park Service representative with SCAT anytime they go to park lands. The SCAT schedule is capricious. Part of it is due to weather, but part seems to be the whim of the moment. Often they wind up checking park beaches, and telling us about it after the fact; or Bud flies all the way out with them, and they never touch park lands. Finally EXXON understands that the Seward Zone is not like the others, and MAC will not sign off on any beach cleanup plan if the agency representative was not present. We get into hassles like lack of intercom communications and are pulled from flights until the EXXON helicopters have federal OAS approval. Every way we turn, the ropes coil around our ankles. The goals are clear enough: keep oil off the beaches and get if off as soon as possible with the least disruption possible. But it often feels like EXXON has different and unstated goals.

As team leader, I am responsible for seeing that the reports of all crew members are written and delivered to the investigators by Monday. The wisdom of Chuck's writing en route becomes evident. His report is ready to be handed over. Sandy will write his in Anchorage and telecom it down. Karen has already written hers and sent it down to Anne. That leaves Bud and I. I am itchy to start on it. As soon as the meeting adjourns, I find my computer and set it up on my drafting table-desk in the Injury Assessment Center. By and large, Peter Paul and I have the place to ourselves. Peter Paul is going through our gear from the trip, cleaning it up and checking it into his supply system. I perch on my stool and squint at the screen of the Compaq. The front of the A-frame is floor to ceiling windows with no curtains, and the morning sun glares directly into the room. No matter how I turn the computer, it is difficult to see the screen. But what the hell--I have a computer and nobody is shoving me out of my chair. Peter Paul finds the untouched bag of Gummi bears. Five pounds of colorful little sugar bruins.

People have not yet discovered the Injury Assessment Center, so Peter Paul and I are pretty much left to our own devices unless we have to go across the street to use the phone. I spread out the maps and notes from the trip and write steadily for several hours. The sun swings south, relieving the heat and glare in the room. During breaks, I deliver film for processing and run errands to the Incident Command Post. Scott Taylor, one of the investigators, has decided we are all working entirely too hard and has set up a Cinco De Mayo party for us at Yvan's tonight.

Lunch time flies by without due notice. But coffee and Gummi bears are some nourishment. Lime ones are particularly good. Peter Paul and I leave little piles of Gummi bears for each other, pulling out our favorite flavors. The red ones are not popular, and we try to pawn them off on the people across the street. They don't understand where this endless parade of bears is coming from. Out of hibernation. They don't like oiled coasts either.

I get the report written by late afternoon. The next challenge is finding a functioning printer. Little tasks like this mean going a mile downtown, begging someone for the use of their computer, fighting with the software to get it squared away and finally, a printed copy. The investigators require the original, signed on the front page. "Original" is a strange concept in this era of electronic files. Then back to the park and send it to the Regional Office in Anchorage via telecommunications. I am still learning the National Park Service software packages, and my clumsiness is frustrating. Finally the report is strewn to the winds, electronically and otherwise. I worked through the Resources MAC meeting today;

Bud attended for the park. After the meeting breaks up, we go home for a few minutes before the party.

    Misty is waiting for us on the porch. It's not much fun for her, fastened to a post by a chain. But at least she gets to smell and watch the spring activities. She's glad to see us and cavorts around the yard. We play chase for a few minutes, but soon I am out of breath, and she heads for the open creek below the house. She comes later when we call, wet and happy from her explorations. Bud and I change clothes for the party. Mexican attire is sparse, but we do our best. My contribution is a belt that Bud brought me from his Baja trip last year.

    The party is in full swing in Yvan's new dining room on the second floor. It still has sawdust on the steps, but the inside is finished beautifully. He has put up some of his Native American art on the walls and windows, and decorated the ceiling in red, white and green. It is amazing to see ourselves laughing together. And no uniforms. Scott invited the second mate from the Soviet skimmer, the *Vaydabgursky*. Our Russian is non-existent, but he speaks broken English and tells of his experiences out on the outer coast with the skimmer. The best technique for skimming oil comes from a Corps of Engineers dredger, usually used for clearing channels and harbors. They turn the dredge upside down and move in underneath a boomed pool of tar. It is fairly successful at removing mousse. The Soviets tried this too, with some success, but the gummy oil clogged the pumps and driftwood and dead birds kept jamming the intake. Cleaning it out must have been a great job. Although they have a capacity of two million gallons, they managed to collect less than 80,000 gallons. By now the oil front has broken up and moved way on down the coast, and their huge skimmer is no longer effective. They will be returning to Russia in a few days.

    After supper, several of us stand talking in the parking lot in the sweet spring evening. Warblers and other little birds are singing their hearts out in the trees, and the creek is runoff full nearby. Although the talk is all of the oil spill, it is a break to be out of the offices, to have children around, to feel the light breezes in our hair. Roy from ADEC wants me to fly with them the next morning, but I hold fast to my precious days off. We can deal with it next week. Bud and I are full and sleepy as we climb into his truck and head home.

I put in a call to Mom. We are planning to dig clams in the morning and go to Anchorage tomorrow night. Mom says that she had a run-in with a clot today. Dad had left the house for a short while, and apparently a clot got stuck. Everything got dark and fuzzy for awhile. But it got loose and she's OK now. I bet the doctors love it.

We have a few minutes of peace and tea before going to bed. No work tomorrow! I fall asleep as full of anticipation as a child on Christmas Eve.

May 6

This morning the early rising is for us. We are planning on meeting our friends, Elaine and Peter, at Anchor Point for the low tide. This is one of the lowest tides of the year, minus 5.6 feet, exposing the beds of razor clams in the clay of Cook Inlet beaches. Stumbling out of bed, we hurry through breakfast, pack gear and load the truck. We picked up Sunny last night, so Bud and I and two dogs are crowded into the cab. Then we head up into the mountains, turning our backs on the dark chaos of Seward. We drive through the Kenai Mountains, along Kenai Lake, down the Kenai River and out into the huge glacial lowlands on the western side of the Peninsula. This is my growing up country, and the retreating snowbanks, dirt patches, bank-full streams and rivers are spring to the deepest part of myself. Every year we went to the Cook Inlet beaches to dig clams at low tide. Mom has an old photo of me in coveralls, sleeves rolled up, great grin on my face, clutching a huge clam with both hands.

We pass through Sterling, Soldotna and Clam Gulch. Much has changed in this country since we left the homestead. I see familiar old landmarks crowded by new developments. The glacial rivers and lakes are clear blue in the spring, fed by snowmelt. Later in the summer, they will be murky green-blue and high as the glaciers melt and feed them silty water. I love the way the sunlight shines through the tossing urgent waves in the rapids of the Kenai River. Then on down the coast of Cook Inlet, closer to the row of volcanoes that dominated my childhood: Redoubt, Spurr, Iliamna, Augustine. This is an active land; within my lifetime all of them have erupted or steamed. This morning their snow-shrouded cones rise peacefully across the Inlet.

We arrive at last to Bud's secret road down to the beach. This is access to set net sites for commercial salmon fishing. Peter and Elaine are close behind us. The tide is still outbound, and we have another hour or so until it's far enough out to expose the really good clam beds. We bundle up against the wind and taking our buckets and clam shovels, we start down the beach. The dogs are going wild, chasing each other through the water and mud. I watch for little pink shells and agates in the rippled sand. As we approach the grey water edge, we start to look for tiny dimples in the sand that mark the clams beneath.

Razor clams are oblong bivalves, growing up to eight inches long. They live in the sand and clay of the beaches, only exposed during very low tides. They live vertically in the sand, long neck extended toward the surface for siphoning water and food. This forms the tell tale dimples in the sand. Their big foot extends below the shell, ready to dig down to China as soon as their sand cocoon is disturbed. The challenge of digging clams is to dig down through a foot of wet clay and sand and grab the clam. But they can dig a lot faster than most humans with shovels. Bud and I prefer the method of going after them with hands, furiously scooping out sand, then working our fingers down their siphon holes until, if we're lucky, we touch the shell. Then a tug of war ensues, human hanging onto a slippery smooth shell with finger tips, clam digging for its life with its great big foot. Success for the clam averages 75%.

Peter and Elaine watch, puzzled, as we locate dimples and demonstrate proper clamming technique. The sand is incredibly cold, and the first holes are painful on hands and arms. By now the tide is out and hundreds of clam dimples scatter the sand. We all dig in, hunched over on our knees, literally up to our shoulders in wet sand, feeling the clam slipping out of our fingers. The wet sand caves in around our arms, and much of the time, we withdraw an empty hand. But some holes are a success for us, and slowly the buckets fill. Bud has watched brown bears on the Katmai beaches digging clams as we do, flinging pawfuls of sand out of massive holes, tossing the clam out with the sand. Eating the shells and running the sharp fragments through their digestive systems must be an experience. No wonder bears are so grumpy in the spring.

We have all the clams we want to clean as the tide turns and starts chasing us back up the beach. We fill the buckets with sea water and make the long trudge back to cars. We are soaked and sandy and numb with cold. But I have a great sense of satisfaction from getting food from the land. Growing up on the homestead, our family grew, hunted, gathered and processed much of our food and warmth. A full woodshed and freezer are my security blankets, engendering in me a sense of well being and completeness.

We eat lunch and toss cracker bones to tired and filthy but oh so happy dogs. Dry clothes are welcome, and warmth slowly spreads through us, hurried along by hot tea in our bellies. Then we go our separate ways to our common task of cleaning clams. Bud and I take the long road to Anchorage. As we pass the cabin, dirt is showing through the gravel banks, and the snow pack is patchy. The entire spring skiing season flew past us this year.

It is late afternoon when we reach Anchorage. We go directly to Mom and Dad's house, intending to clean clams there and make a huge pot of chowder. But as we go up the stone stairs to the front door, there is no welcoming tap on the window, no lights on inside. The hospital bed dominates the front room--and it is empty! Peering into the garage, the car is gone. Alarm rises in me as I envision an emergency trip to the hospital, racing the effects of the blood clots. Hurried calls to my sister and brother result in endless rings, neither of them is home. Dazed, Bud takes me up the hill to my own home, which is also empty, with no messages on the recorder. Finally I call the hospital and ask for Eloise Spencer, and the receptionist puts me through without a pause. Relief floods through me when she answers the phone. We talk briefly. Apparently, the doctors want her under closer control while they're playing with her blood consistency. Reminds me of mixing pancake batter, getting the right thickness for cakes. I chastise her for going to extremes to get out of clam cleaning.

Bud and I turn to the chore of divesting each clam of shell and sand. It takes four hours to clean the clams we dug in an hour this morning. There are simply no short cuts to getting the pervasive sand out of every orifice and cranny. Our fingers are wrinkled as prunes, and we are weary as we finish the job and count the sacks of clams with satisfaction. Then a welcome hot shower, quick snack for supper and fall into bed.

May 7

We wake slowly and late in the Sunday morning light. Frankie and Patty are both gone and we have the house to ourselves. We revel in the luxury of a full night's sleep and slow morning hours. Hot chocolate and the Sunday paper while watching the light on the mountains across Cook Inlet. Slowly we bring ourselves into the day. A few phone calls to touch base with friends and family. We may as well be on another planet for all the contact we've had with familiar people. Steve and Romney Ortland ask us to stop by during the day. Steve says he's finally finished our wedding present.

Later we are welcomed into their home, their puppy a whirlwind around our legs until we put all dogs into the back yard. Romney serves us strong rich coffee, and we talk of ordinary things and of Steve's latest paintings; he's working on airplane and mountain images. The evening light he puts on the mountains of Turnagain Arm is glorious, just like flying home on a fall night, racing the setting sun to the surface of Lake Hood. Then he hands Bud and I each a wrapped parcel, and we open them to find a pair of paintings; skiers winding through the mountains past a snowy open stream beneath a pink-washed sky of setting sun. Originally a large image, he has cut it in half and framed each side. I am in one, and Bud the other. When we live in separate towns, each has one for our walls. When we live together, they can hang side by side. It is an incredibly thoughtful and appropriate gift for us, recognizing the realities of our living separately for now and the dream of a home together.

Later we swing by Lake Hood so I can check the plane. The winter-long ice is nearly gone. Normally this time of year I would be anxiously patrolling the shores, bugging John to be ready to put the plane back in the water. But for now the Cub sits grounded on the shore and I have no idea when I will be able to fly her this summer. We drive across town to the hospital. Again Mom is surrounded by machines. She is bored with the whole procedure and ready to get on with spring. Instead she watches the birch buds swell through the windows, her room filled with the smells of antiseptic and the sounds of the hospital intercom instead of warbling bird calls. I have brought her some tapes and compact discs. Loon calls go in first and their haunting cries echo in this foreign environment. Our conversations are light and superficial. We are all going through experiences too profound to risk to words. Maybe we don't even have the words yet.

When Dad shows up, we arrange to have supper at our house that night with John Craighead who is visiting for a few days. Leaving the hospital, Bud and I run a few errands, getting supplies we can't find in Seward. Home again, we clean the house rapidly, and I make a huge pot of clam chowder. That evening a large and noisy group of people gathers in our front room for supper. A table full of food magically appears, then disappears. Many of these people are involved in oil spill activities. Some are going to the beaches, but many more work behind the scenes in town in education, on Frankie's book, on a nationwide hotline--each of us filling niches we never thought possible, spreading the word as far as we can. I gather some calmness and perspective from Dad and John. Between them they have watched many events of this magnitude pass by: nuclear testing at Amchitka, oil development on the Kenai and the North Slope, grizzly bears in the garbage at Yellowstone.

Later after the kitchen is cleaned and our guests have left, Frankie, Patty, Bud and I sit in the calm of the front room with tea, catching up on our lives of the past weeks. Patty will soon be going out to the beaches, working for State Parks. Frankie is deeply involved in the coordination of her book about the oil spill. Bud and I leave oiled samples with them, for the Visitor's Center, for talks in schools, so that others can see a small sample of the reality from the coasts. We all go to bed early, craving sleep after the weeks of sparse rest.

May 8

Bud rises in the early morning light and heads back to Seward before I get out of bed. By 8:00 he will be at the morning briefing in Seward, two and a half hours away. I am spending another day in Anchorage to catch up on errands. Shortly after Bud leaves, I too get up and dive into the day. Frankie has transferred my midden upstairs, and I sort through the piles to pull out critical items. Bills have all come due again. Rent and electricity and phone seem to have little relevance in the world of boats and radios. We have considered renting out my room for the summer, but I need some place where my belongings will stay still, where hopefully I can still find things where I left them.

I go through my closet to select spring clothes. During the last month, I have gotten so tired of heavy dark clothes, and I long to wear bright colors and pretty clothes again. I take an armload of pink and blue shirts and white pants. I am coming to know that I have to learn to live in the madness of Seward. Learn how to find or provide the nurturing I need for the long haul. I select items to last the summer: a few books, my sewing machine, toys for Misty. The trappings of a normal life to sustain me.

Then down into town again. At the dry cleaners, they bring me my wedding dress encased in flimsy plastic. The women exclaim at its beauty, and I marvel again that I actually danced in this dress scant weeks ago. The sequins catch the sunlight as I gently lay it in the front seat of the car. Bud and I keep saying that we're going to dress up again and go out for a night on the town, but neither of us can forecast when that day may come. I stop by Keller's and pick up the enlargements of our wedding photos. The memory of that happy day sweeps over me, such a gathering of support and love around us. I am humbled when I think that if we had delayed it as much as one week, we probably wouldn't have had the wedding. Most of us would already have been pulled into the oil spill.

Late in the afternoon, I stop by the office to pick up stuff to take to Seward. I am having a lot of difficulty getting the most basic office supplies, so I take a box into our supply room and grab a few pens, tape, paper, staples. I just ignore the bulging in-box. Then a quick stop at home to leave the wedding dress and another stop at Mom and Dad's to leave wedding prints. The sun is sinking below the Alaska Range as I head down the highway to Seward. Evening light is high on the mountains around me as I drive around the Arm, then deepens to dusk up the pass and through the mountains to Seward. I arrive in Seward in time to share a late supper with Bud.

My small glimpse of a normal life flickers out as he goes over the events of the day. We have been told several times to persevere until we are "over the hump." From the refuge of my time away, I see that there is no "hump," only long continuing work for months ahead. The emergency was over as soon as the oil hit the shores. Oil can be removed from water, but all of our activity has very little effect on the oil silently pushing up into the rocks and the beaches. But we continue to create a pressure cooker in a well intentioned attempt to make a difference.

May 9

The morning passes in a whirlwind of finishing up details from the last trip and beginning planning for the next trips. We still need to complete the oil survey on the Aialik Peninsula that we started on the *Spirit* voyage. Then another in-depth survey the week of May 22nd to map oil contact, fisheries, water quality and cultural resources assessment prior to beach cleanup. Sandy calls, asking if I have seen his float coat. It disappeared during the unloading of the *Spirit*. A hurried search among our equipment does not turn up his faded, tattered float coat. We also need to order a replacement for a complex and fragile piece of equipment borrowed from the University and cracked during the last voyage.

Other details roll over us. The *Kenai Ranger* and the *Malibu* will be headed out on Wednesday to set up the camps for the back country rangers in McCarty Fjord and Paguna Arm. Bud will be gone for three days on this trip. The investigators are frantically working on finishing their first report. Boom is being pulled out of James and McCarty Lagoons today, although no one in the Resource MAC knows why. A new slug of oil is reported coming out of Montague Straits and heading our way. The miner at Surprise Bay requests a special use permit to go to his mining claims and make his radio system available to the bird rescue crews. Helicopter and boat availability changes hourly. It gets frantic as we attempt to match needs with conveyances. The MAC is pressing us for names of additional beaches for Type

A surficial cleanup. ADEC and I will coordinate another list for VECO, even though they are barely started on the first list of six beaches.

In mid-afternoon I get a call from Paul Haertel in the Regional Office. He is preparing a status report of costs and accomplishments, both to date, and projected throughout the summer. He asks me to write a summary report for him of the work in the Seward Zone and our projections for the rest of the season. He needs it in two days.

I am tired and frustrated by the time Bud and I call it a day and head home. I fix supper while he packs gear for his trip out to the coast the next day.

May 10

We rise to a cloudy day. The Regional Office has set up an Area Command staff and brings another Incident Command Team to Seward to help the park. The new Area Commander for Seward leads the usual ICT meeting. All the logistics information of yesterday is reversed today: our summer long helicopter is assigned elsewhere, and boat availability is scrambled. The communications system between the outer coast and town still staggers along, but is not functioning. Several trips have been made to locate a radio repeater which was set out last summer, but the record snowfalls have apparently buried it, and searches are fruitless. At 10:00 A.M. I meet with the new Area Commander. I give him a copy of the monitoring plan, since it is the overall plan for our activities. He immediately wants to know the schedule of boats, aircraft and helicopters, numbers and kind of people, support inflatables, outboard engines, and a myriad of other details for the whole summer. Sitting in his office, with a copy of the summer's planned work, I make a list on the fly for the oil tracking and resource assessment work.

I am already fatigued from the concentrated effort of scheduling by the time I get a chance to start on the report I promised to Paul. Much of the information I need is in reports of other scientists and minutes from the MAC meetings. I shuffle through haphazard stacks of papers which were piled in my corner during the move, trying to find copies of these key documents. I finally begin to write as best I can, leaving blanks to fill in with critical dates and names. Later I leave to try to locate these data at the park office and the ICT headquarters downtown. When I return after lunch to resume the report, I discover that someone has been in there moving furniture and unplugged my computer. All the morning's work is gone. I am discouraged as I try to reconstruct the report, then break for the Resources MAC meeting.

The Resources MAC group has grown so large that we have moved the meetings to the conference room of the local fire department. New faces appear daily, often with great ideas about how the oil spill should be run and what should be done. The meetings are getting eruptive as contrasting egos and agency viewpoints come together. Jack Sinclair has been unanimously appointed as our leader and is a calming influence on us, keeping the meetings on track and on time. The new people from Outside with training in oil spills are slightly contemptuous of us who are blessedly inexperienced with oil; and those of us who have been working on the spill from the beginning and know and love this land are losing patience with trying to explain the situation over and over again.

In addition to all the overload at work, the timing for moving to Bud's new house begins to get tight. While I was on the *Spirit* trip, Bud signed the papers for the purchase of his new house. He has given notice on his apartment, and with the incredible housing crunch in town, it has already been rented to others. We come down to a few days in the midst of the madness to pack and move all of Bud's belongings, clean his apartment and attempt to establish order in his new house. Each evening this week, I work late into the twilight, packing shelves and drawers into boxes and loading the car. At lunch time, I take the load to the new house and pile the boxes in a corner. Bud's worldly goods are hopelessly scrambled. When he returns from his trip, wet and weary, it is a job to find a pair of clean socks.

May 11-12

Dozens of strangers move through our offices and boats and beaches. Although their help is badly needed, they usually have three-week stints, and the learning curve varies from a few days to two weeks. Those of us with continuity and knowledge of the land are called upon again and again. Strong egos and conflicting objectives begin to clash. In our fatigue we treat neither ourselves nor each other very well. And on the streets outside our office, hundreds of people stream by, arriving from all over Alaska and up from Outside to cash in on the VECO wages of $16.69 per hour. Working late at night in my office before the plate glass windows, a group of intoxicated men press themselves against the glass and noisily watch me.

VECO finally begins Type A beach cleanup. Type A is collection and removal of surface oily debris only, without any disturbance of the surface. Type B, which comes later, involves the disturbance of the surface and includes the techniques of hot and cold water washes, shoveling, tilling the beaches and use of chemicals in an attempt to speed up oil degradation by bacteria.

As the cleanup progresses, VECO schedules and actions become increasingly secretive. When we are told to be on the dock for a boat leaving at noon, we find it departed at 7:00 A.M. Hundreds of people invade the beaches of remote bays. Every action brings controversy, and wild stories and rumors abound. There are multiple reports and samples of the flaky "white stuff" that we found on the *Spirit* trip. In one story, the white stuff dissolved a hole right through a gull. A cleanup worker is taken to the emergency room with a hand covered with blisters after handling it. Large slicks of it have been reported in Aialik Bay and Granite Passage, extending one half mile long and several hundred feet wide. EXXON steadfastly denies use of dispersant. When the samples are returned from analysis by NOAA, we are told at the Resources MAC meeting that it is "animal fat." If that is true, we have a lot of dead animals beneath the sea.

At the direction of the Coast Guard, the National Park Service provides armed rangers for all cleanup crews to patrol park beaches and watch for spring hungry bears who may stumble into the madness and to watch the cleanup activities, ensuring that important resources are not impacted by the crews. Now we have to scramble to have firearm certified rangers available. The park only has three people who are firearm qualified; one of them is on crutches, the other two are already doing two or three jobs at once. A call goes out to the Park Service nationwide for assistance and a steady stream of rangers comes from all over the country. They are given a lecture in bear behavior, handed a shotgun and sent out to the coast to provide a Park Service presence for the VECO cleanup crews.

In the turmoil, I continue my plans for another oil mapping voyage to the coast. My resource orders for equipment and logistics get lost or confused in the fray, and each task is often redone multiple times. The administrative structure changes constantly, as the ICT framework tries to accommodate new responsibilities and tasks. The table of organization seems to shift daily. On some charts I work for the park as the Injury Assessment Coordinator. Other charts show me in the bowels of the ICT. Even Anne's position as Superintendent moves. It is very confusing when the system expects certain paperwork and behaviors of each of the roles. Each of us already has huge workloads in other areas: track the oil, evaluate the impacts, coordinate with other agencies and answer the multitudes of requests we receive. And although we are real glad to see a full time ICT arrive to help, it is the third set of people we have to bring up to date on our activities of the past six weeks.

Many of us working on the oil spill seem to have become addicted to being busy. Frankie calls it "activity therapy." We maintain the edge of fatigue where we find numbness from emotions which would swamp us. Much discussion, scurrying around, logistics planning without end to send an army to invade the waters and shores of the coast. The bureaucracy in town is well intentioned; we feel a deep urge to do *something*. But hours are spent cleaning each live oiled bird while thousands of bird carcasses wash onto the shores.

May 13-14

By the time Saturday rolls around, it is a do or die effort to finish the move to Bud's new house. The SCAT team is scheduled to work park beaches this weekend and Bud and I are on call to fly with them. Fortunately for us, the weather is marginal, and SCAT sits on the ground all weekend. All day Saturday, we pack and move massive loads to the new house. The skis have been stacked in the corner like cordwood and are nearly a whole load. Then another load for kayaks and associated equipment. Several loads for books. The dogs follow us restlessly on every trip in and out of the apartment and sniff the corners in the new house. Late Saturday night, the new house is piled high and the apartment is forlorn, all the accumulated dust and debris revealed to the light. We leave it in the evening light, murmuring stream below the hill and happy memories of our early months together.

Earlier I slipped over to Yvan's, and he made huge ham sandwiches for a picnic and added a foil-wrapped package of heavenly chocolate eclairs. I grabbed a bottle of wine during the packing and found a few broken doggie bones. All of these go into my pack. Bud accepts my offer to take him to dinner but looks puzzled as I bypass downtown and head south to Lowell Point. Understanding dawns when I lift my pack out and calling the dogs, we head down the beach. We find a few oiled kelp leaves, but that is the only trace of contamination on the beach. VECO has been diligently patrolling and cleaning all the beaches which are road accessible from town, so that no scrap of floating mousse is apparent to the visiting public.

We settle down at a drift log and open the wine and sandwiches. Misty and Sunny leave off romping in the surf and watch our every move until the dog bones are passed around. The gentle surf slurps on the sand as the tide advances. High snowy mountains ring us, with Seward out of sight around the corner. A land otter scampers down the beach and slips into the water. For a few precious moments, we are out of the frenzy. We lick the chocolate frosting off our fingers and walk hand in hand down the beach. The coming evening pushes the last of the sunlight up the mountains across Resurrection Bay and squeezes the rosy light into the sky above the peaks. The dogs are joyous in the low surf, Misty swimming for tossed sticks, Sunny sprinting madly along with us, and then both of them wrestling in the wet sand. We savor these sparse minutes free from oil and clinging responsibilities and the avalanches of questions and worries and tasks which have overrun our lives.

That night we take the foam pad out of the back of Bud's truck and spread out our sleeping bags on the floor. The unfamiliar noises of traffic and neighboring dogs keep pulling me from sleep during the night. The delight of the dream of a new home is blunted by fatigue and the confusion swirling around us. Next morning we push ourselves awake. My camping grub box furnishes sooty pots for hot chocolate while Sunny and Misty explore their new neighborhood. Then we return to the apartment and spend several hours cleaning it from stem to stern. Finally we are finished and pull the door shut behind us. The last item taken is the phone, since we are on call, but luckily it has been silent.

Over at the new house, we look at the mounds with dismay. Somewhere in the unidentified boxes are the trappings of daily living. Bud starts in the garage, I take the kitchen. But later when he comes in, I turn around and find that he is switching drawers and shelf contents to suit his patterns. Finally I leave the effort and concentrate on locating my duffel bags and finding a corner for them. I know he hates my piles in the corners, but neither does he want my sense of organization. I wander around the yard, finding new leaves poking through the winter debris and envision the rock garden that will bloom later. I have no sense that I belong in this place, even though I am scheduled to live the summer here. In the midst of this unrootedness, I am developing a deep longing for a place of my own, a place I can return to, a nurturing, homing place.

Misty reflects my uncertainty, shadowing my meanderings about the yard. Finally I go back inside and by late afternoon, Bud and I have brought some small order to the house. Peter stops by to make the SCAT non-flying report and gets a tour. "So Bud-like," he gives his verdict of the tiny house. It is like a Hobbit house, small and cozy, covered with wooden shakes. Pegs in the entryhall hold our colorful array of raingear and bunting jackets. But after one glance at the confused kitchen, he asks us to join himself and Elaine for supper. The quiet evening in their home is a welcome relief from the turmoil of moving. When we go back to our foam pad bed on the floor, we are both very tired. The moving has been stressful and physically exhausting. Even though we didn't fly with the SCAT team, we haven't had a real break.

May 15

We awake early to a new day, stumbling around the house trying to find the light switches. When we leave for work, Sunny protests her new pen in the yard. The Injury Assessment Center is full and quiet when I step inside, but nobody responds to my good morning. When I left Friday, it was nearly empty, but over the weekend the office furniture I'd requested for the scientists has arrived and been set up. However, a whole new crew for the ICT has also moved in with people from all over the country hauled unceremoniously up here to help us out. The Center is full of dividers, the open space broken into little compartments, and all my papers and materials are again dumped in a box by the movers. In the back corner, I find an unoccupied desk and a rickety chair. I try to find my files and photos again to resume the task of coordinating the scientific work and planning the next oil mapping trip. I get a cup of coffee from the park office and Peter Paul shows up to help break the ice. Slowly we all tentatively reach across the echoing floors to each other.

When the building was used as the office for a tour company, they had big tubs of flowers out on the porch. I have had my eye on those tubs for a week, waiting for warmer weather and a spare hour to get to a nursery. Flowers by the door would be welcoming in the frenzy this summer. But in the afternoon I glance out the window and see the tubs being hauled away and dumped in back.

All day strange people circulate through the Center. Emphasis is shifting to support the rangers who are to accompany the cleanup crews to the beaches. When I go through the warehouse, looking yet again for Sandy's lost float coat, I push aside the racks of Mustang suits and am confronted by a wall hung with shiny shotguns. I begin to feel like the park has been invaded by an army. The people who come probably feel like they have been kidnapped to a strange land. The Center becomes crowded and noisy as more and more people are brought in.

Bud and I call it an early day, leaving at the end of normal working hours for the first time since the spill work began. We take a short walk up the back trail on Mt. Marathon behind his house. The trail is steep and we climb slowly, out of shape from the lack of spring skiing. But the muddy, organic earth slippery beneath our feet smells rich with the promise of growing. Spring birds flit among the branches of huge spruce, twittering all the while. The dogs tear through the woods, peering anxiously up tall trunks at distant squirrels. I still can't understand how they can charge through the underbrush without getting snouts full of devil's club spines. Soon Bud's nesting instinct calls him to the task of unpacking, and we turn back. For supper we have fillets of fresh halibut, surprise gift from a fisher friend. The evening passes quickly as we work our way through boxes, trying to find new niches for Bud's possessions. A small sense of normalcy pervades these hours, giving me hope that we can make a sane life in the midst of the oil spill hysteria.

May 16

Arriving early at work, I find that my hard won phone has once again been moved to another desk, and my furniture rearranged in the night. I am spending a phenomenal amount of energy and time just trying to find and track important items.

Then late in the afternoon, as I am busily tying together the frayed logistical strings for the upcoming oil mapping trip, a member of the new ICT physically pushes me back into the room as I am leaving on an errand, harshly telling me not to talk with my colleagues. I am stunned. Somewhere in the past two weeks, my role in the oil spill has gone from coordinating the injury assessment activities to being a gofer who gets pushed around. When I try to talk with Bud at home that night, he tells me I am imagining things. I crumple inside, no longer able to withstand the anguish that is assaulting me. Running blindly out into the spring evening, I find myself half way up Mt. Marathon, sobbing and sobbing; Misty leaning against my back and anxiously licking my face. Tidal waves of pain and agony sweep over me, tossing me about without direction. I am being swept downstream in a turbulent river, without any sense of control. Much later, I look about and find that I am sitting in acres of yellow violets. I pick one and wrap it in cow parsnip leaves. I will take my car and go into the mountains, so I can sleep on the ground tonight. Desperately, I need to feel her hardness beneath the length of my body. Submerge myself in her smells and bursting greenness. Find some small thread of sanity again, before facing another round of the frenzy.

The house is empty when I make my way back down the mountain. Bud is out teaching kayak and water safety to the new coastal rangers. I find a large scrawled note from him, apologizing for yelling at me. I am too exhausted to move now and crawl into our bed on the floor. Sleep is no longer rest.

May 17

The next morning I have an early meeting with SCAT and ADEC about condition of oiled beaches and to make cleanup recommendations. SCAT has finished initial reconnaissance of seal and sea lion pupping rookeries and wants to whip through the sensitive anadromous fisheries streams. I sit down with the ADEC women who are flying the oil monitoring to go over our work in the Seward Zone and produce a composite map. SCAT has also requested a list of beaches for invasive Type B cleanup. This is a different issue. The National Park Service does not give wholesale authorization for machinery and disturbance on park lands, but wants to evaluate the characteristics of each oiled area and associated resources before making decisions about cleanup. I put SCAT off until I can consult with Anne. VECO already has a list of over two dozen beaches in the park for Type A cleanup, and I know they are nowhere close to finishing those.

Various forms of the media swarm through Seward, trying to get to the coast where possible, talking to people who have been out there, constructing stories from the wild mixture of fact and fantasy prevalent in the streets. Anne, Peter, and Bud all appear regularly in the newspapers and on national television. For a time, it is the only way our friends and relatives Outside know what is happening in our lives. A reporter from the *New York Times* calls in the evening while I am working late. He also wants to get on oiled beaches, but the weather is 100% horrible: freezing wind-driven rain, tempestuous seas, squirrely winds, and fog. As we talk, he asks questions about what I have seen on our voyages and the impacts of the oil on the natural ecosystems. I explain the whole scheme to him: food chains, impacts to individuals, populations, the web of life and energy transfer, short term events and long term impacts, seasonal variations, ocean currents. He gets a real earful of Ecology 101 and Early Oil Spill in Northern Marine Lands. Then something within me stirs, and I tell him: "I don't know if this has a place in your story. But I want to tell you of the impacts to the people here, of the personal impacts on me." And I tell him of being a mega-educated scientist, Dr. Page, standing on the bow of the *Shaman*, crying as I simultaneously watch a bird die and collect specimens. He is subdued as we finish the call, and he returns to the National Transportation Safety Board hearings, and I to my report. But those are the thoughts that he writes up, the quotes that appear in papers literally all over the country. We are slowly beginning to understand that the impacts extend beyond ecology and economics, reaching into the realms of our spirits.

All of us who are heavily involved in the work in Seward are affected, but we manifest it with different emotions. Each of us has become fully involved with the work, as the oil spill events gobble up our normal lives. There is an ambient sense of excitement, knowing that our work is vital, a commitment of energy and creativity to the task at hand. But woven with the challenge, we harbor a secret suspicion that what we do really doesn't matter. The oil is in the land and the ocean. We dab away at the surface and record the results. We give it the best of our hearts and minds and souls and bodies. But our efforts are trivial compared to the magnitude of the event. A heavy wet blanket of fatigue and stress smothers each of us.

Bud is angry, and the rage courses through him with every blackened sticky corpse, every bureaucratic smokescreen, every corporate lie. Another becomes addicted to the high in the eye of the hurricane of energy. Another withdraws from the scramble, knowing that this is not his place, husbanding his energy for other tasks. Others come with a combative, militaristic approach, determined to "win," insensitive to the nuances of land and people. Some hibernate in a haze of alcohol, denying the reality of the madness all around. Violence comes and we see one among us with bruised eyes. Many are able to salve their pain by working in the bird and otter rescue centers, finding some small solace in cleansing fur and feathers and literally breathing life into a newborn sea otter pup. And for some of those, even that feels futile. Those on the beaches, paid in plentiful EXXON dollars for their dignity and health and energy, kneel in filthy raingear wiping rocks or stand horsing heavy hoses to wash beaches and accumulate their grief and rage and greed. And in the wealth, or just the hope of wealth, drugs and alcohol abound, and the crime rate in Seward explodes 300% above the previous May.

And I become a black hole of grief and pain. My land is hurt, and the anguish courses through me. Each assault on her sears like acid splashed on my soul. I break at the end of my tether, and nearly drift out on wind tossed seas. From this place, I can no longer consciously chart my own journey. Small gifts come to me: a new friend, a longed for massage, full moon rising over Resurrection Bay, totes full of halibut heads for cheeking. But they do not begin to allay the agony.

May 18

Today the entire staff from the park is scheduled to take the *Spirit* on a day voyage to Aialik Bay. This annual introduction to the park is part of the training for summer seasonal employees. We all gather in the grey morning, bringing our picnic in boxes to the dock. The decks are crowded as Jack Scoby, co-owner and skipper for the day, backs the *Spirit* out of her slip, and once again we are headed south out Resurrection Bay. The clouds hang over the mountains, and the seas are calm. Jack starts the trip with his usual tour sights. Several sea otters obligingly float and feed and pose for photos. A bald eagle lands near her nest, a nanny mountain goat and very young kid graze and cavort near the water's edge. The permanent staff members take turns with the microphone, each speaking from their expertise. Bud explains the glaciers as we pass Bear Glacier and points out sea birds and other wildlife. I explain about oil strikes on the shores, cleanup and skimming methods, point out signs of oil on logs and rocks. Later I get to discuss early blooming flowers and vegetation patterns. We make a side trip to the Chiswell Islands. The air overhead is a swirling screaming mass of seabirds, courting and building nests. The puffins are late arrivals, having flown in since the last *Spirit* trip in early May. They have the aerodynamics of a bumblebee, huge brightly colored beaks and tubby black and white bodies. They skitter along the surface, wings and bright red feet both flapping frantically, until they are thrown into the air at a wave crest, bounce a couple times and are airborne. I'd fail an FAA check ride if I made a take off like that in the Cub.

We finally head up Aialik Bay. I have a strange sense of isolation as the familiar land rolls by. For the first time in weeks, I do not have an overload of immediate chores demanding attention, and I am disoriented by the sudden change. I feel disconnected from the enthusiastic seasonals, many of them seeing this magnificent country for the first time, looking forward to an exciting summer. I feel like I have already done a full summer's field season and am overwhelmed as I look ahead to months of crushing work. I am disturbed by the direction of the new ICT and the struggle to find a place for my office and the work of the injury assessment. At last we arrive at the Aialik Bay Ranger Cabin which will be home to the summer rangers. We shuttle everyone to shore and open up the cabin. All looks in good shape after the winter.

I wander north along the beach while the crew lights the charcoal fires and sets out dinner. Automatically, my eyes follow the tidelines, checking for tar balls in the seaweed. The snow is still deep under the alders above the beach, but the runoff stream flows off the cliff and across the beach. At the far end, I crawl onto a flat boulder and sit in the weak sunlight. The bay waters are quiet, the *Spirit* resting in the patterned reflections of mountain and cloud. The mountain rises right behind me, fern fiddleheads pushing up through last fall's withered fronds. The devil's club leaves are still tightly wrapped in buds, bristling with thorns. And peeking through the humus, yellow violets lift their blossoms. Right on schedule, spring is arriving in the land, but my heart is out of sync with the seasons. For the first time in my life, I look forward to summer with mixed emotions. Anticipation of warm days and back country explorations combine with the dark work before us, tracking the spread of oil and counting the carnage from its passage.

Silence from the cabin indicates that food is spread out, and the crew has already dug in. Sure enough, I return as many are starting on their second round. Later, my friend Ida and I retrace the beach to cut willow twigs for marshmallow toasting. It is late afternoon when we clean up and ferry gear and crew back to the *Spirit*. The run back to Seward is long and quiet. After awhile, I seek my favorite spot on the bow and wedge in under the railing for the rest of the trip.

May 19

Friday passes in a blur, as though the *Spirit* trip was a fantasy we didn't have time to dream through. The intricate details for the upcoming oil mapping trip and the summer's work swarm over me. Sandy's float coat never materialized, and the order for its replacement got lost. At the Resources MAC meeting, SCAT presents yet another request, this time for a list of moderately oiled beaches. ADEC reports a fresh slug of oil and mousse on the Pyes, and sheen and mousse are still spreading along the coast. VECO wants to put a fuel cache on the old airstrip at Beauty Bay, then they want all-terrain vehicles to collect the sacks of debris off the beach. SCAT also wants a National Park Service representative to accompany them on overnight boat trips, even though much of the coast they intend to visit is not park land. Both Bud and I are scheduled to be on other trips next week, and we have no backups for this task.

Wearily, I am bounced from task to task, giving each one just enough to keep it in the air. Like a marathon runner, I feel like I have hit the wall and totally expended my energy. I have no more reserves. Every unexpected change, every new nuance, every lie or broken word, every disrespectful action, brings a surge of adrenaline flooding through my body. Without exercise and rest, I am assaulted with stress toxins building up in my system. I can no longer concentrate. Usually I can easily track several things at a time, but now I lose focus when new matters intrude on the current project. I am constantly beset with mercurial winds which threaten to destroy my work.

Later in the day, talking with Lindy Lawson, a friend in the Regional Office, her words filter whole through my fog and register. "Page," she says gently, "someone else can do it for awhile. Call Paul and ask him to replace you for a couple weeks. Come back to Anchorage and work here and get some rest, and then you can go back." She looks up his number for me, and although it is after 5:00 on a Friday night, Paul is still in his office. Without pause or question, he hears my request and tells me to return to Anchorage for two weeks. Russ Kucinski is also working late, and Paul asks him to take over my duties. Russ is one of the crew for the next oil mapping voyage on the *Spirit*. He agrees to become crew leader for the trip and coordinator for the injury assessment work. I arrange to meet him at his home in Anchorage Sunday morning, to go over work to date, maps, and procedures.

I feel badly about abandoning the work here, even for a two week respite. But I absolutely know I must leave Seward to survive. Anne appears upset when I tell her, but she knows that Russ will be able to continue my work until I return. When I tell Bud, he says he understands that I have to get out of Seward for awhile, but I don't sense that he knows the intensity of my need.

Bud and I spend several hours tonight down at the fishing docks bent over huge metal totes cheeking halibut. Halibut cheeks are a delicacy, prime meat in the sides of the halibut heads. But carving them out is tedious, cold, slimy work. Evening draws over us, dark bluegreen skies at midnight, touched with the last hint of rose from lingering sunset. The full moon rises from behind the eastern mountains, gently drawing above the ridges, shimmering light path stretching across the waters of Resurrection Bay to our feet. A tremendous sense of release starts to trickle through me, knowing that I will have a break from the frenzy and chaos. The evening is full of richness: plastic buckets brimming with delicate halibut meat, intense moonlight glowing over dark mountains. Scattered lights on the bay are incoming vessels, glad for a calm passage into Seward. Even the seagulls have settled down, no longer screaming at each other over scraps, but perched on roofs and light poles, muttering softly to themselves. Finally Bud and I call it a night, taking our wealth home to pack away for winter. Our clothes are stiff with slime and reek of fish, so we hose them down and leave them crumpled on the lawn.

May 20

We sleep beyond the alarm clock this morning, savoring quiet time on the floor. The dogs are delighted that we are at nose level and insistently push at us for playing. Rising, we face buckets full of halibut cheeks demanding cleaning, bagging and freezing. The work is time consuming but rewarding. Soon rows of halibut join the clams in the freezer. Such bounty.

I spend the afternoon organizing and documenting my work for Russ. Peter Paul fills my lists of supplies and equipment for the upcoming oil mapping voyage. I gather maps, forms, film and files, so Russ can follow our work from previous voyages and tie his next voyage with it. Plans are in the mill for several other scientific projects, and I write down the status of each.

Afterward Bud and I head for the docks again and delve headfirst into the totes for a few more halibut heads. It seems a shame that the cannery turns them into dog food. At home we clean our latest loot, saving out the biggest for supper.

May 21

Bud and I awake to rain pelting the metal roof and dripping off the eaves. I pack a few essentials to take back to Anchorage for my break. I plan on being back in two weeks, so I leave most of my gear at Bud's house. I would like for Bud to break out too, but he doesn't feel the need and is immersed in the oil spill work plus his usual spring duties of training back country rangers and getting them set up on the coast. We have a brief goodbye in the rain, and Bud sends me off with his usual admonition to drive carefully. Misty and I head north in the rain, wipers a steady rhythm against my tumbling thoughts. I keep a pad on the seat beside me, scribbling notes about subjects to discuss with Russ. The last snowbanks are melting away from the shadows as the car climbs the pass and beyond the cabin at Manitoba Mountain. Streams rush away, intent on spring breakup duties. Early leaves are a faint green mist in sheltered nooks. Scattered dandelions, grasses and jacob's ladder bloom on the roadsides. The trip passes in a blur, my emotions smothered in grey fog that matches the clouds filling the mountain valleys. Rain is still pouring down as I arrive in Anchorage and follow Russ's directions to his house.

We spend two or three hours together, and I leave him with a box full of maps, notes and materials. Briefly, I go over the past two months work and tasks projected for the next two weeks. Russ seems fresh and ready to meet the challenge. Later I drive up the hill to my home. Misty sniffs out all her old corners and vanishes up the mountain for a muddy exploration. I poke around in the piles in my room in dismay. Wedding remnants are dumped with discarded socks, all thrown in a pile in the corners while frantically searching for warm clothes to take to Seward weeks ago.

Tonight Celia Hunter, grandmother of conservation movements in Alaska, is at our home for supper. This is my first family dinner with Frankie and Patty since before the wedding, and I have missed the love and support and camaraderie of my household. The talk and laughter bounces back and forth in the evening light, although I can find no words to join the conversation. For dessert we have dishes of ice cream. When mine is empty, I go to the refrigerator and bring the cartons back to the table. Filling and refilling my bowl, I try to find sustenance and nourishment to last a summer. At bedtime, Celia hugs me and tells me I have worked hard, and not to feel badly about needing a rest.

On May 22 I am in my Anchorage office at 7:00 A.M., dressed in my pretty pink dress and ready to tackle mining issues. But people stop by, or draw me into talk, and I cannot stop the tears. Later Nancy calls it the "pink dress syndrome," where we come back from a devastating event, denying that anything is unusual, and think we can just go on with life.

I have two weeks to recover and rest, and I set out to fill the holes in my life. Wearing pretty clothes--I buy an expensive skirt, not because I need it, but because it swirls when I turn and is bright red. Eating green salads. Visiting friends and family. Seeing Ketki for a massage. Getting my hair cut. Sleeping. Hiking in the mountains.

Soon my calendar is full, but by late in the week, it is evident that my efforts at healing are superficial. I am going through the motions, but the internal void and physical fatigue continue unabated. Every morning I struggle to rise and go to work and find it difficult to redirect my focus to usual tasks. When I take Misty for evening walks behind the house, I veer off the trail within the first quarter mile and fall asleep in the sun, waking hours later dazed and cold. I feel almost frantic about slowing down and resting. I stop in to visit Paul and try to describe the conditions on the coast of the park. I am determined not to cry in his office, but my words are sparse and broken, and tears brim in my eyes. Despite my efforts, Paul notices and recommends that I see a stress counselor.

Four days later, the counselor diagnoses traumatic stress syndrome and exhaustion. He recommends "having someone take care of me." My blue guiding light flares in alarm. He means putting me in a mental hospital. I know, as I know little else in this darkness, that I will become certifiably crazy if that happens. Finally I remember that I can go to the Manitoba Mountain cabin with a minimum of logistics. The counselor calls Alex and explains that I am on sick leave for at least two weeks. Leaving his office, I do not even return to work. I get a load of grub, an armload of books at a bookstore, and head home where I collect Misty and clothes.

I spend over two weeks at the cabin. Mostly Misty and I are alone, although Bud comes for a weekend and friends stop by to visit. I sleep 12 to 14 hours a day with nightmares on the rampage. When awake, I sit in the doorway and watch the sun go around, reading fiction from other places and times. I chop a little wood, haul some water from the creek. Log oiling the cabin is the only chore of maintenance I complete. During the second week I take long hikes into the surrounding valleys, exploring the mountains in their spring newness. Flowers are bursting through last fall's leaves and streams are bouncing down mountain sides and canyons. Misty gets into porcupines twice, requiring a rapid trip in and out of Anchorage to see the vet. I brought comfort foods, treats I had not had in a long time. But I am not hungry and eat very little.

In this time, I start to heal. My body begins to rest, to recover from the exhaustion and toxic poisons. I know that I cannot return to Seward immediately but need more time away from the oil spill to continue the healing which has begun during this precious time in the mountains. My friends Ketki and Al encourage me, gently at first, then adamantly, to write a journal of what I have seen, and how it felt. While I am at the cabin, the words began to flow out of their own accord.

The summer months pass in a mosaic of introspection and tentative reaching out. I had every intention of going back to Seward, but by mid-June I am still physically unable to work full-time. After returning to Anchorage from the cabin, I slowly resume my tasks in the Regional Office. Alex makes the space and gives me the support for this time of healing. But many days tears start to flow as I sit at my desk staring out my window. I leave the office and go to the Coastal Trail or to the mountains of the Chugach State Park behind my home and walk and walk and walk, letting the sun and rain and wind soothe my pain. My huge reservoir of sick leave drains rapidly. I begin the field work for reconnaissance of placer mining districts in the National Parks. I walk wonderful lands, diverse and beautiful, and begin to plan for their reclamation and the healing of scars from disturbance.

I am blessed with friends, some who don't know my history, but sense the pain and encourage me to talk about it. The words are jumbled, jerky and unclear, the images all scrambled as I tear the top layer off the churning vat and try to describe it. And they take me to other adventures, giving small respites from the oil and chaos I left in Seward. Logan explores old mines with me, explaining in intricate detail how all the machinery worked. With Roseann in Denali National Park, I rejoice to see the alder seedlings she planted growing sturdy and strong in the gravel tailings. I go with Nancy to an ancient land and wander the ridges between granite tors and soak in old hot springs late into the summer night.

In July Bud and I go back to the park coast to collect vegetation data from the plots Mike and I set up in April. Full summer is in the land and we have spectacular weather the first half of the week. We walk around the shorelines, tentatively reaching out to reconnect with each other and this land we love. It has been nearly a month since we have been alone together. We feel as battered as the beach we walk in Beauty Bay. Thirty days, sixty people, thousands of red garbage bags full of greasy gravel. VECO has "cleaned" this beach and left it in silence, if not peace.

I had left the insane chaos six weeks before. Bud remained, working night and day, continuing the tasks that require his knowledge and absorb his dedication. He spent two weeks on a seabird survey, bobbing against the wave washed cliffs in a Zodiac, counting the remains after the devastation. Day after day he went to the coast in helicopters and boats. Each rocky cliff, each gravel beach, each eagle nest and sparkling stream is a treasured memory from his earlier years on the coast. He has kayaked her waters and climbed her mountains and slept in her rain in simpler times. Now each slimy smear is a personal assault, compounded in town by government indifference and EXXON distortions.

I mourn the loss of these irreplaceable first months of our marriage. Although no promises were given, there is a part of me that wanted "happily ever after," at least for awhile. Instead both Bud and I were thrown without warning into a war.

We have become split off from each other, moving carefully in separate bubbles. We came to this marriage without a long history together, built our vows on the faith that we would grow and change together, make of these years an exploration of ourselves and each other and our world. But the magnitude of the changes in our land and our work has overwhelmed us and our relationship. Each of us is so impacted that it is difficult to spare energy and support to the other. It is clear that Bud cannot hear of my pain nor hold me while I cry. When the grief leaks out of me, he turns with harsh words and runs. I cannot listen to his anger and frustration, for it triggers my own. Each of us has to find our own paths for now, and later, our healing. So we gingerly and gently move around each other, thankful for the brief times together, nurturing the hope of saner times, treasuring our love in the faith that it will survive. Our wedding words come back to me again and again, "Recreate this day in joyful times. Remember it in hard times." And so the hard times came first, and I travel back to that evening and remember the celebration of our commitment, and know how absolutely right it feels to stand with this man.

The vegetation analysis and report for the July trip with Bud is the last oil spill work I do for months. While I am in Seward before the boat trip, I come to know that I cannot return to full-time work on the oil spill. The bureaucratic system there is poisonous to me, and I cannot survive another toxic drenching from my reactions to it. I draw a 30-mile radius around Seward and to Bud's dismay, refuse to go inside it for several months. I had completely expended my emotional and physical energy and drained even the reserves. I had run the tanks dry in my little plane, and the engine sputtered, coughed, and was silent, the prop whirling in the wind as I looked for a place to land. I managed to set her down in an open place right side up, but with a few scratches in the wings. I spend most of the summer and fall patching her up.

EXXON spends the summer throwing money at the oil spill, trying to cover the pervasive blackness with green. During the height of the cleanup, they employ 11,000 people, 1400 boats and 85 aircraft, using 1.4 million gallons of fuel. The cleanup crews are supplied with 100 miles of boom and 302,000 pairs of rubber gloves. Estimates of oiled coastline vary widely. Between one and two thousand miles of coastline have been contaminated with oil originally contained in a 987-foot tanker. EXXON changes their rhetoric over the months, starting with a vow to clean up the entire mess, to treating the beaches, to making them environmentally stable. Their reports of expenditures mount up, first one billion, then two billion dollars, but cleanup crews report rampant waste and inefficiency. The surge of money into the economy does not buy good will or forgetfulness. One season of wealth does not buy a livelihood. And people in coastal towns become split, as some choose to work for VECO and earn money to pay off boats and planes and lavish vacations, while their neighbors choose to not take the work and face a winter of boat payments on minimal incomes.

We followed the invasion of tarry tides with another invasion of technology. And we are leaving footprints which may last as long as those from the oil. Boats chase down oiled otters and birds, the crews capturing them with fishing nets and hauling them into town in cages. Cleanup crews pile thousands of red plastic garbage bags full of oily gravel on the beaches. Four wheelers zip along the shores with trailers, hauling the sacks to the water to load onto landing craft, leaving tracks in the soft mud. Another crew hauls the bundles of debris over a delicate land otter trail from one cove to another, leaving an eroding muddy gash in the wildflowers. The onslaught of noise and energy and people is incredible to a land which usually resounds to the rhythms of the tides and seasons. Bud likens it to two oil spills: the first one of petroleum and the second of humans. And I think the later may have wrought as much change as the first.

In June the *EXXON Valdez* leaves the embattled Sound, heading south for dry dock in California. A slick of fresh oil continues to spin out behind her wake. On September 15, EXXON pulls out their final boats and cleanup crews, citing approaching winter storms and safety concerns. By summer's end, EXXON's media office reports that they have worked on all oiled beaches, leaving "nothing neglected."

Estimates of treated beaches vary widely, from less than 500 miles to over two thousand.

I reexamine my own life, trying to become more aware of my actions and the results of them. The issues are much larger than finding a way of life that is less dependent on petroleum products. It is about making conscious and responsible choices about my uses of resources. Not to despair because my presence impacts the earth, but to become aware of each moment, and make choices, rather than defaulting to the easiest path. My work on the oiled beaches has given me a profound understanding of some of the costs of my lifestyle.

After I leave the oil spill work I move slowly and gradually back to health. My emotions have a very thin veneer over them, and in the sudden slowness, I deal with them as they surface. Walking and sleeping on the land, I become centered again, although in a different place and with a different balance. My roots to the earth, torn loose so violently, reach back tentatively at first, then hungrily. I become nourished by the land again, growing fat and glowing in the falltime richness. I emulate the bears storing reserves for hibernation and go to the salmon streams and alpine meadows. I splash in the creeks and run through the flowers and roll laughing down slopes of Labrador tea until the world spins in my dizziness. I push blueberries into my mouth with both hands, spitting out the leaves and grabbing for more. Curious caribou peer over the knolls at this strange human-bear creature and move on. Gifts of salmon come to me, a few from the migrating hordes. At freezeup, Bud and I take a canoe and go to Skilak Lake and paddle her around the shoreline with ice fingers growing out into the still water. Cranberries are frost-bitten and soft and stain my fingers and knees. The trumpeter swans are gathering for migration, waiting for the north wind in the passes to leave the country. As we cook supper over the fire, the flames are reflected in the blazing sunset covering the sky, and the sparks spiral up to become the first twinkling stars.

I follow the patterns of the land as she uses summer quiet and winter storms to heal her wounds and adjust to the changes wrought by the oil on the water. Both my body and heart will bear the scars of the spring's events. But I gain much understanding of myself and the earth, and in the process, accumulate some wisdom.

December 27, 1989
Seward, Alaska

I have come to Seward for a couple days to extend the long Christmas weekend with Bud and to finish writing the first draft of my journal in peace. Soon it goes to the editor/publisher, and the process of turning a very private record into a public book begins.

I sit in an upper room facing both computer screen and a window overlooking the Seward small boat harbor. Yesterday was bitter cold with north winds over 40 knots, gusting through the rigging and scuffing the water's surface. All morning I watched two sea otters diving, feeding busily, rolling every minute to clean their fur. They were oblivious to the harsh winds sending dark cats paws around them and building white caps in the outer bay. Now the harbor waters are absolutely calm. Snow has been falling heavily for several hours, piling over two inches an hour. It falls straight down, without a breeze to direct its course. The snow blanket lays on the water's surface, not dissolving, nor sinking, but accumulating slush over the entire harbor. A few ducks and gulls are wintering here, having missed the fall migration to warmer climes. I watch them chug through the thick wet snow on the water, white feathers breasting soggy snow down. They leave a web of paths behind them, like miniature ice breakers. The tide is inbound, ripples nearly imperceptible at the shore edge, but gradually melting the snow blanket and pulling it out to sea. Dimly through the moving veil, I see the otters again, feeding offshore, soft snow landing on their heads and washed overboard with each cleansing roll in the ocean.

The oil spill work and impacts are far from over. But the land is gathering her energy to herself, hurling huge waves at the rocky headlands and exposed beaches. And in this hiatus of snow and silence, I solidify my own healing. And that is as much as each of us can do. We cannot "clean" or "treat" or even "stabilize" oiled lands. At best we can sop up the dripping excess and become aware of our choices, as we turn to our own healing.